# Shades of Gray

A Mother's Guide to Work and Family Choices

# Shades of Gray

## A Mother's Guide to Work and Family Choices

Lynn Hennighausen, M.S.

Beaver's Pond Press, Inc.
Edina, Minnesota

ISBN 1-931646-21-X

Library of Congress Catalog Number: 2001099221


Printed in the United States of America.

04  03  02  01    5  4  3  2  1



Beaver's Pond Press, Inc.

5125 Danen's Drive
Edina, MN 55439-1465
(952) 829-8818
www.beaverspondpress.com

*Shades of Gray* is dedicated to
my Mom and my Grandma
Hoida, the two women who
most influenced my life.
It is dedicated to my Dad, whose
confidence in this project helped
me through some rough spots.
It is for Rick—meeting you was the single
greatest thing that's ever happened to me—
and our children, C.J, Ricky, and Sydney.
You're the best.

# Table of Contents

## Shades of Gray:
## A mother's guide to healthy work and family choices

# Preface

## When you have a choice:
## My story

I'd like to share my story as an example of one woman's journey through the labyrinth of change we all face as our lives with children begin. I offer my comments only as an example of universal issues. The decisions I made with the help of my husband, Rick, have led my family and me on a good path. My goal in sharing is to provide a bit of insight that may help you find your right path.

Each of us experiences a number of defining moments in the course of our lives; those major transitions transform us in ways that change us forever. For me, there have been a few: moving away from home, meeting Rick, having three children, and making the decision to radically change the course of my career to stay home with my children. Thankfully, I have that financial option. Making the decision to stay home with my children has been the longest, most difficult internal struggle in my life to date…and I will never be the same. This transformation did not come easily for me, and I fought it every step of the way.

Before my oldest, CJ, was born, I worked 60 hours a week; worked out six or seven days a week; and belonged to a book club and a card group. My husband and I were involved in a variety of activities. Everyone marveled at how much I did and how well I did it. How did I do it, they'd ask? It was no big deal, I'd say, feeling quite proud of myself. Go, go, fast, fast, fast was my way of life—pack in as much as you can; don't slow down. I thought I had the world by the tail.

EEERRRRR…to a screeching halt. When I was eight months pregnant, on medical leave for two weeks with six to go, Rick told me I looked more rested than he'd ever seen me—and I was eight months pregnant! Thus began the search.

I was forced to step away from the pace, and I'm thankful for that. Society rewards the woman who works full time, has two children in seven different activities, runs marathons, cooks dinner every night, and keeps a clean house. It's craziness! I knew my journey toward slowing down and simplifying my (our) lives had begun. What a journey it has been.

## GREATEST CHALLENGES

As I battled myself about the best choice for me and for my family, I felt overwhelmed. My husband was traveling three or four nights each week; CJ was two years old; we had just moved to Minnesota. I had worked in a professional career since finishing graduate school years before and enjoyed my professional identity. My career was very much an expression of who I was.

One of the biggest reasons I quit working was because Rick's travel schedule was not going to change, and one of us had to lend constant stability to our family. In many ways it felt good, as if it was the natural choice. It's difficult to have a career when your partner cannot share in responsibilities like driving to/from childcare, staying home with sick children, bringing a sick child to the doctor, or getting them to baseball on time. And the truth was, Rick traveled too much to predictably rely on him for those things. I can say all that now, but this truth eluded me for a long time.

My major roadblock to staying home was a naïve view of a stay-at-home Mom. I remember wondering what stay-at-home Moms "do all day." I was one of those women who scoffed when a co-worker had to leave a meeting early to pick up her children or deal with a child's illness. And if I decided to stay home, what would Rick and I talk about at the end of the day? He'd talk about clients, meetings, company politics; then I'd talk about the load of laundry I was able to do that day, CJ's new word, how much fun we'd had playing in the snow. So what, I thought. I was worried that Rick would find me boring. No more good work stories from me, I thought—the characters, the politics, the scandals! Yet, there was something inside me calling to be the core of our family, to be a stable force for CJ. It's evolved into so much more.

Once I made the decision to stay home with CJ, the struggle was far from over. I felt an overwhelming sense of guilt for having fun during the day. My work shouldn't be fun like this, I thought. It felt wrong. Surely Rick wasn't having this kind of fun during his workday.

And I missed the feedback a workplace provides. At the office, I'd work on a project and it was completed. Someone said, "Great job, Lynn," or "Here's something to think about next time." At home, projects don't get completed; they cycle—beds, meals, getting kids dressed, vacuuming. And the cycle is sometimes measured in minutes, nanoseconds even! The whole house seems to come undone in the blink of an eye. Each day, I get up and start all over again. No one tells me how I'm doing with my children like a manager or co-workers assess performance at work. CJ, Ricky, and Sydney frequently express their opinions, of course, but that's not *exactly* what I am looking for.

Feeling financially dependent on Rick began as a major issue for me as well. It was really difficult for me to spend "his" money. (I'm proud to say that I've gotten over *that*.) Not only was "his" and "mine" becoming "all his" an issue, but living on "just his" was a transition in its own right. We are fortunate not to have significant money-related issues, yet moving from two professional-level salaries to one did change our lifestyle. On a cognitive level, we knew that right away, but it took awhile for our brains to catch up with our day-to-day spending habits.

Those of us who have a tendency toward perfectionism add an additional challenge to the reality of staying home. Nothing about staying home is perfect—not the house, not me as a parent, not our children, not relationships. Learning to cope with that truth is difficult. It was easier to strive for perfection in the workplace because I could periodically come close. Learning to let go, however, has taken some of the pressure off.

Rick, on the other hand, is a perfectionist in nearly every sense of the word. Recently, he was looking for a pan to cook dinner. He opened the cupboard and was frustrated with the disarray he found. He asked me how much more time it would have taken to put a pan away in the right place instead of jamming it in. He told me that it surprises him because I'm such a perfectionist in my work and I have such a strong work ethic. He just couldn't understand how "stuff like that" didn't bother me.

After reminding him that we have a one-year-old whose nickname is Velcro Baby and two other children under the age of seven, I told him that I have had to evaluate priorities over the last couple of years and make split-second decisions about the importance of each issue as it arises. Dealing with Sydney or Ricky or CJ that second must have taken precedence over proper pan location. Then I suggested that he places the same weight on ALL tasks, from proper pan replacement to submitting a $4-million proposal to a client. My new weighting system helps keep me sane.

## FINDING PEACE

During my journey, my roles evolved as I accepted myself. As you will read in Chapter 4, each of us has a number of roles, from partner to Mother to daughter, spiritual being, individual, friend, volunteer, and employee. It is possible to separate and acknowledge each one, even set goals for them individually, and then recognize yourself as an integrated woman. When I first became a stay-at-home Mom and someone asked me what I did, it felt demeaning to say I was a stay-at-home Mom. It was foreign and invalidating. My identity is not as separate as it once was. It is unmistakably intertwined with my roles as Rick's wife and as the Mom of CJ, Ricky, and Sydney. And that's OK, I think. I'm proud now to say that I'm home with my kids.

Feeling good about being a stay-at-home Mom must come from within. Before I was home with my children, my sense of fulfillment came from other places, whether it was through my job, school performance, or some athletic accomplishment. As I look back at my transition and transformation, I'm sure I had suffered some level of depression after our move to Minnesota and was actually treated for a postpartum depression following our middle child's birth. Both experiences were frightening in a real, raw way. As an individual perceived by others as having it all together, learning that I didn't always have it together was a stunning realization.

I've learned that I must be happy and content with myself, my actions, my parenting skills, my ability to organize our home. Rick's sense of humor and sensitivity helps, but they alone cannot sustain me. In an environment where our hands are always busy with our children while our minds are searching for intellectual stimulation, there's plenty of room for self-doubt, as well as unrealistic, even irrational thoughts about our families, friends, children, partners, and expectations of ourselves. How ironic. One of my greatest concerns about being absent from the workplace was that I wouldn't reach my potential. I was searching for personal rewards, kudos, public acknowledgment. What I got instead is far more personal growth—really discovering my true being—who I was meant to be from deep within.

## KEYS TO MY SENSE OF FULFILLMENT

My mainstay is my relationship with Rick. Our marriage and friendship have transcended to levels beyond any I thought possible. Rick and I do a lot with our children. It's important and it's fun. But those relationships with our children exist naturally as a result of our strong, lasting marriage. Rick's support and love for me are enduring. Often he can't understand what I am saying, thinking, or feeling, but he stands by me, supporting me in the place I am that day (or that hour or even that minute). We laugh a lot—sometimes he laughs and I cry. I have energy for him because I don't feel the professional stress or frenzied pace I used to feel. He's my great supporter. He knows that his life is easier because I am the Chief Executive Home Manager. He understands that I stay home not so that we have a super-clean house or great meals on the table every night. I stay home so that we can raise our children according to our standards and expectations.

A strong support system and my own individual interests are also keys to my feeling fulfilled during these years that I am home with my children. I talk to friends every day. I'm lucky enough to have a "back-door neighbor," the kind you had when you were growing up. It seems there was always a house where you knew the family well enough to walk in the house with a quick knock on the back door.

My friends and I frequently meet at a park, spend time at one of our homes, or find an indoor activity in the winter. It is so very comforting to know that I have friends surrounding me—to help me if I'm struggling, to be there to laugh with me, to pitch in if I need anything, to reconnect, to recommend a pace-check. To feel validated, it helps a great deal to interact with other women who have made similar parenting choices.

I also interact and feel supported by my friends employed part-time or full-time. We share our worlds with one another and provide comfort in the difficulties the other experiences in her choice. We become momentarily envious of the other's world, but we know in our hearts that the grass is not always greener.

The last important element for my feelings of success during these years at home has been finding time for me and doing something that's just mine. I hire babysitters. When Rick's gone, my children are in bed at 8:00 p.m. Making time to meet my own personal needs is a day-to-day struggle but perhaps the most worthy of all struggles. After finding that time, I am a better individual, a better parent, and a better partner. Exercise is a very important part of my life, so I keep it a priority. Having coffee with a friend or with Rick or going for a run quickly rejuvenates me. Going on a date with Rick is a breath of fresh air. Writing is my work and I love it. Each week, I set attainable goals for myself, and their accomplishment feeds me. Ask any truly content, satisfied woman about refreshment, and she will say that she takes care of herself; she finds time to re-energize.

## TAKE TIME

The decision-making process, as well as the outcome, have deepened me tremendously as a person. The medical leave I was on before CJ was born in 1992 was truly the first step in my long journey. Only by distancing myself from the pace and detail of my life could I consider my life's treasures: family, the opportunity to watch my children grow and blossom every day, involvement in our church, the chance to follow through on the kind acts I only had time to think about before. I believe that the key to forming a good conclusion is allowing yourself and your partner the time, distance, and objectivity it takes to think through all possible choices. This is an emotionally charged issue. It cannot be made because your partner, brother, Mother-in-law, or best friend thinks it's the best way. Your personal answer doesn't lie in my decision, your Mother's decision, Madeleine Albright's decision, or Mrs. T. Berry Brazelton's decision. It lies inside you—inside your heart. Listen.

We live in a society that rewards perpetual motion and the scheduling of every last available moment. We must allow ourselves time that is unstructured and without parameters, constraints, or deadlines. When we have ample time for that, we allow our mind to wander a bit, tear things apart and put them back together—maybe in a slightly different order. Things become clearer. We must then trust that the decisions we are making are right. We must learn to step off the treadmill of life and allow ourselves to make good decisions—good for us and for our families in this moment of our lives. A Zen philosopher, Krishnamurti, says "We are all confused about our many problems and lost in that confusion. Now, if one is lost in a wood, what is the first thing one does? One stops, doesn't one? One stops and looks round. But the more we are confused and lost in life the more we chase around, searching, asking, demanding, begging. So the first thing, if I may suggest it, is that you completely stop inwardly. And when you stop inwardly, psychologically, your mind becomes very peaceful, very clear."

## MY GENUINE SELF

And now? I am at peace. I have FUN with my kids. Part of the job description I keep for myself is to be fun and to have fun. It is an important piece of my legacy. My true, unabashed personality now shines. At work, I wore a suit and gold earrings and ran only for exercise. Never hopped. Didn't sing much because I don't sound very good.

It's taken awhile, but I seldom wear gold earrings anymore—I wear salamanders, fish, turtles, hoops, and Gumbies! I wear blue jeans. I hop, I jump, I skip...because it's fun and it makes my kids laugh! We have a science club. I sing loudly and animatedly and the kids like it! I get to eat Teddy Grahams and popsicles and drink juice bags. We make pudding finger paints. I'm a good Mom; I'm a fun Mom. I have found my sense of creativity (primitive as it may be). "I'm a knight today, Mom. Could you make me a knight mask?" "I'm Batman, Mom—make me look like Batman, pleassssse," Ricky says. Those words terrified me at first. CJ will say, "Mom, who is the fastest football player in the world?" or, "Will you pitch balls to me?" It's great. I feel like my priorities are in the right place.

For now, I am the strongest link in the chain that will pass on Rick's and my values, morals, standards, and expectations. We believe that our role as parents is to raise three responsible children to be respectful, accountable, secure, stable, sensitive adults who make a contribution to the world in which they live—with a sense of humor. I want to influence their very character. I find it essential to teach our children the importance of refreshing oneself, of time for reflection, spirituality, and introspection. I want my children to understand how important it is to feel whole, so I must model wholeness. The importance of exercise, good nutrition, relaxation, and reflection must be modeled to be effectively passed on. Children must learn how to reach out to people in need—friends and strangers. I want CJ, Ricky, and Sydney to always feel that I'm there for them—physically as well as emotionally for now; emotionally forever.

Is staying home hard? Do I still struggle? Just ask Rick and my friends! However, it's different for me now. Until I felt confident and secure about my role, I struggled with my children at times and wondered at the same time why I'd made this choice. Now, I still struggle with my children at times, but I no longer wonder why I am where I am. I have a clear picture of who I am and of the role I play; I have a clear sense of purpose.

# THE FUTURE

Regardless of the choice we make as women and Mothers, I truly believe that this choice is one of the most personal we are faced with. Universally, we ask, "What's best for me? What's best for my partner? What's best for my children?" The answer cannot be the same for each of us, as we are each fundamentally different as people and within the relationships we share. We must respect each other as women and parents—all struggling for balance, strength, and happiness.

When my children are older than they are now, I'll have another career, but climbing the corporate ladder, making a lot of money, having power—those aspirations are long gone. What I need now is flexibility and personal fulfillment because that's what works for me and for my family. My priorities feel in order for now—to meet the needs of my whole family, including me.

I wish you luck in your decision. Listen to your heart, and it will be right.

# Acknowledgements

I always wondered how acknowledgements got so long when I read a book. Now I know. From the women I interviewed, to my friends who watched my kids while I wrote or had another meeting or interview, to my personal Advisory Board, to the employees of Caribou Coffee Lodge in Woodbury, MN who re-filled my coffee cup many times in the dozens of hours I used it as an office, to all the courageous women who paved the way for me to have the choices I have today, thank you. To Milt Adams at Beavers Pond Press, Bette Frick who edited my book, Jan Stanton who proofread it, Jaana Bykonich and Jack Caravela from Mori Studio who designed my cover and the format—thank you.

It is virtually impossible to thank everyone individually but I will do my best nonetheless:

Martha Bullen, Linda Carrigan, Jessica DeGroot, Bob Drago, Dawn Erickson, June Erickson, Marti Erickson, Ph.D., Amy Gage, Mary Mahoney, Anne Hennighausen, Della Henricksen, Mary Dee Hicks, Ph.D., Cheri Hoida, Jeanne Hoversten, DeDe Kelly, Linda Kelly, Gail MarksJarvis, Reverend Mary Keen, Deb Martin, Marlene Muenchau, Marty Mumma, Brenda Novotny, Cheryl Prescott, Kathy Richardson, Tammy Schafhauser, Kathleen Smith, Barb Smith, Sarah Storvick, Ginita Wall

And, of course, thank you to the more than 200 of you who gave me your time to share your stories about your work and life choices, how those choices are working for you, and what sort of balance you feel in your life. This book exists because of you.

# Introduction

*I cannot say whether things will get better if we change;*
*what I can say is they must change if they are to get better.*
G.C. Lichtenberg

Lee works as the Marketing Director for a large bank. Her career has progressed over a period of ten years. She is in a position of influence and is highly respected at a level most women never reach. She is where she always wanted to be, yet something doesn't feel right. Her 7-year-old, James, is struggling in school and at home. Lee wondered if being home more would help. Her husband, Jim, has a high-paying job as well, so Lee could step away from her position if that's what is best for her and her family. She sees this as the biggest decision of her life.

Margo has been home full-time for ten years. A nurse by training, she's ready to re-enter the workforce because her children are in school all day. But now she's faced with re-educating herself—and she knows she'll get the least desirable hours since she has no seniority at the hospital in town. Why did they have to relocate for her husband's job, anyway? Maybe she should have kept working part-time all along.

Jennifer just had her first baby. She always thought she would go back to work full-time after she and her husband, Curt, had children. After all, she had worked her whole life to earn her way to her current job. But now, looking at Lucas, she just doesn't know anymore. She never expected to feel this way.

The changes these women face are mirrors of today's society. Change is everywhere. We cannot always predict it. We do not always embrace it. One thing is for certain, though: As women and Mothers, we will face many crossroads. Your crossroads may include the birth of a baby, your children's going off to school for full days, your adolescent wanting to stay

1

home alone after school, a job opportunity for you, a job that isn't working for you anymore, a partner's job that isn't working for him anymore.

Like Margo, Jennifer, and Lee, I have made significant work-family changes since having children. I moved from full-time to part-time employment to being at home full-time. I learned that my husband, Rick, would support any decision I make because he knew I had the whole family's best interest at heart.

I also discovered that I wasn't alone in my search. I learned that virtually all of us as women and Mothers struggle with work- and family-balance issues. The good news is we have more choices than any women before us; the bad news is that with those choices comes the difficult responsibility of finding the right path.

## RESEARCH

Sometime during my transition from work to home, I decided to write this book. I wanted all women to know they are not alone in this journey. Since 1997, I have interviewed more than 200 women, some fully employed; some employed part-time; others who telecommute, are self-employed, or are home full-time with their children. All had at least one child at home. I asked Mothers all sorts of questions about their choices regarding employment and parenthood, their level of satisfaction with their choices, their sense of balance, and their awareness of work-family-related change on the horizon.

In addition, I spoke with psychiatrists, industrial psychologists, and others in the work-family arena. I asked mental health professionals about the process of change, re-evaluation, and re-ordering. I talked to them about where we are as women and Mothers and what they see as the key issues for women at the dawn of this millennium. We have so much to learn from each other. So much to learn—and so much acceptance to offer.

There are some general observations that surfaced from those interviews:

- Women must take better care of themselves.
- Women feel tremendous guilt with regard to their children. Women blame themselves for any and all problems children have.
- Women see the relationship with their partner as a crucial piece to achieving successful work-family balance. A woman's ability to communicate her needs and her partner's ability to support those needs are necessary if anyone is to achieve a balanced work-family life.
- Women are the catalysts for change in the workplace. As a result, more employers are recognizing the importance of providing necessary changes. Simultaneously, women recognize the need for more men to jump on board and talk about how important family is to them.
- Most women who are employed full-time feel a sense of imbalance, yet they continue along the path of least resistance as they did before having children. They do not recognize a need to evaluate their options.
- Women who say they want to be home full-time with their children but insist they cannot afford it need to take a second look. I met families who live on $35,000 a year, even waiting to buy a house or a second car so one parent can be home with their children.

From my interviews, seven universal issues emerged—issues that I believe all women as Mothers experience a number of times in their lives whether or not they recognize them at the time:

1. Changes in your personal identity
2. Evolution of your relationship with your partner
3. Others' expectations of you
4. The need for reasonable work-life balance
5. Long-term career implications of work-life choices
6. Your need for financial dependence
7. Maintaining a sense of personal wholeness

## USING *SHADES OF GRAY*

Each universal issue is detailed in its own chapter. Read those chapters that speak to your current concerns. Challenge yourself to look at the difficult issues while making sure you don't skip one because it frightens you.

Following the development of the issue, you will find *STO-RIES*, composites of the women I interviewed and the points they made time and time again. There may be one or two profiles in each chapter that will cause you to think, "YES, that's me!!!" Choose those profiles to reflect upon, using the list of "Points for reflection" as a springboard to examine your personal situation. Write in the space provided between the points, make notes in the margins, or keep a companion journal. Based on the results of your analysis, develop an action plan for yourself.

## CHANGE IS HARD

Self-evaluation and change are not easy. It may often seem easier to follow the path of least resistance and complain than it is to do something about your situation. Change moves us from a point of comfort into an unknown, placing us at risk. We ask ourselves, "What if I make the wrong decision?" "What if I don't like the change?" There is safety in familiarity even if we don't like it.

I saw this truth when I interviewed Keri, who had been a top-level marketing executive in a highly demanding company. She has two young children. For three years, she knew she didn't want to continue working full-time. She felt she couldn't make a change although she was unable to articulate her reasons. Having only one income might stretch their family resources, but they could handle it. She finally confided one night that the reason she hadn't made a move was that she was too scared. She was highly visible and well-respected in her job and afraid of whom she'd become if she didn't have that. Her life would be so different. Would it be full enough? Would she be bored?

Keri's long journey placed her finally at home with her children, consulting about 10 hours each week from there. Fear can be paralyzing, but Keri got past it; she's thrilled to be with her children and is happy with her choices. "People will do anything, no matter how absurd, in order to avoid facing their own souls," Carl Jung reminds us.

## DEVELOPMENT PIPELINE

Industrial psychologist Mary Dee Hicks, Ph.D., first pioneered the "Development Pipeline," a method for making positive personal change. Dr. Hicks subdivides the process of change into four steps:
- Insight
- Motivation
- Reflection and searching
- Committing to a plan

The tools you need to help you carry out these steps will be described in the *STORIES* portion of each chapter.

Insight ☛ Motivation ☛ Reflection/Searching ☛ Commitment to a Plan

### INSIGHT

Insight means that you have realized that something in your work-family life is off-balance. You may know it intuitively, or perhaps the evidence is becoming clear. The very fact that you are reading these words indicates some level of insight on your part. Look at the list below and check any of the statements that apply to you.

❑ I have voluntarily opened *Shades of Gray*.
❑ I sense that I am on some sort of personal journey.
❑ I feel torn too often about where I'm spending my time.
❑ My partner and I talk about how "something has to change."
❑ The things my kids say lately or the way they act doesn't feel good.

❑ My priorities just don't feel in order.
❑ I'm not taking care of myself.
❑ My partner and I feel too disconnected too often these days.

If you didn't check a statement on the list, close this book and pass it on to a friend. My guess, though, is that you are on a journey, and this is a good place to start.

## MOTIVATION

For positive change to happen, you must have some incentive to make a work-family change in your life. What's motivating you? Is your job too all-encompassing, leaving too little time for your family? Did you receive a job offer, an opportunity, that is very difficult to pass up? Do you feel guilty leaving your workplace at 5:00 p.m. because corporate culture practically mandates you stay until 6:30? Are you feeling restless at home, in a rut and searching for more? If something doesn't "feel" right, then it's worth evaluating.

In this step, you must search for what you really want for you and for your family. Evaluate your priorities. Make sure you and your partner are on track to reach your goals as a family.

## REFLECTION/SEARCHING

You know that it's time to make a change. You're ready, you're motivated. It's time now to consider all of your options and gather information from various resources. What steps do you need to take to change the situation?

Support groups, personal trainers, web sites, books like this one and others, friends and family, partners, life coaches or counselors are just some of the many resources available to you.

Take advantage of the network you build, but remember that only YOU know what's best for you.

Going back to work after being home? Think about whether you need to take some classes. Would it be helpful to conduct a few informational interviews? If you are considering moving from full-time to part-time work, you'll need to make a plan, write a professional proposal, and have a conversation with the appropriate people at your company. If you think telecommuting twice a week is the answer, write your proposal and present it. Hoping to stay home full-time for awhile? Better run the numbers and see if it's feasible; make sure your partner is encouraging you to make this change. Set up a strong support system for yourself.

## Find the time to reflect

In our busy, busy lives, it is imperative to find enough time to reflect on the changes you are considering. How do you think best? Get the support of your partner, other family members, friends, or babysitters so you have the time to consider all of your choices.

There are many different styles for reflection. What's best for you? Below is a partial list of ways you may best listen to where your heart is leading you:
- Go away: Can you take a few days, a week or two, to physically remove yourself from your current day-to-day life? Find a place where you can really think?
- Keep a journal.
- Think in a long shower; linger over a cup of coffee; go for a run.
- Spend time with your partner discussing your thoughts.
- Talk to a friend.
- Meet with a counselor or personal coach.
- Speak with your religious leader.
- Develop a "Support Team"—make yourself accountable to several peers by telling them what you're thinking. There is energy and self-responsibility in "saying it out loud."

I know some of these suggestions seem extreme. A sabbatical, a couple of weeks away alone, counseling—these are big commitments. And right now you may be thinking, "That's nuts. I can't take that time away. How could I? It would be so selfish! How would I present it at work? At home?" I simply encourage you to challenge your assumption that these options are impossible. They may be selfish and drastic, but they will help you on your journey which, in the end, will restore a greater sense of balance not only for you but in the lives of all of those who surround you.

If none of the options above will work for you, put your kids to bed one night a week with a good book, cassette tape, or drawing paper. Or get up before anyone else in the morning to spend time with yourself. Make it a priority. Schedule it before cleaning your house or washing your car or doing the next load of laundry.

Find the method that works best for you. If you are a journaler, journal. If you like quick phrases, use the space provided. Write in the margins; write in the STORIES. If you like to talk things out, seek out your partner, a friend, your pastor, or a counselor. But do talk or write or reflect.

### COMMIT TO A PLAN

Let your support system know how they can help. Rely on them when you are tempted to second-guess your decision. Once you commit, don't look back and wonder "What if...?" Such thoughts will only sabotage your process. Finally, give it a chance to work. I talked to women who, once they quit employment, needed more than a year to feel good about their choice. A woman who has been home with her children for ten years will have a major transition to re-enter the workforce. Someone moving from full- to part-time employment may struggle with workload issues for a while. Be patient.

With the appropriate balance of your intuitive feelings and the objective information you have gathered, the right decision will come.

## FEEDBACK VS. ADVICE

Throughout the book, you will read about the importance of listening to your own voice and filtering others' expectations of you. Overt and covert messages we receive from society, family, friends, and the workplace can be destructive to anyone's decision-making process. You must be secure enough with yourself to filter these messages so that you are certain that your decisions are made in your own best interest.

At the same time, asking particular trusted individuals for specific feedback about a topic can be helpful in the process. For example, my friend Polly was recently offered a great job opportunity at a new company. She e-mailed five people she trusted highly and asked their opinions, fully expecting a broad range of suggestions. She received the responses, integrated the advice into her thoughts and feelings, and made a decision. Only a very secure woman can ask for advice knowing she may not hear what she wants to hear.

## ADVICE FROM A FRIEND

I asked women from a variety of work situations the question, "What one or two pieces of advice would you give to a woman who is deciding how much, if any, she wants to be employed while she (and her partner) raise a family?" Here are some of their responses:

☎ "It's important to search your soul and your heart and honestly answer the question, 'What's best for me, my child, and my family?' And if you listen to your heart, the answer will be there, if you're willing to hear it."

—Kathy

☎ "A change [affects] not just me, but my whole family. [Considering a big promotion has forced me to say:] 'What is important to me now? What can I put off, that I can get to later?' The job is No. 1—not that I love it more than my children, but it is my primary responsibility, as breadwinner. The children are the No. 1 love in my heart, and they deserve as much of my conscious presence as I can give them."

—Amy

☎ "RUN—as fast as you can!!!"

—Tammy, with humor

☎ "With my experiences now as a woman who's stayed home with her children for eight years, I would, if I could do it again, find a flexible part-time job where I could be stimulated intellectually but my family could still be number 1."

—DeDe

☎ "'Life is brief and fragile; do what makes you happy!!!' I love this quote and have had it framed on my desk or dresser for over ten years. Make sure your decision is the one that makes YOU happy, because if you are happy, everything will fall into place."

—Dawn

☎ "Consider the entire family when making your decision, and by that I mean consider each member individually, as well as the whole. Many times the decision is made for the children or for the Mother, but it needs to be made considering every individual and every relationship—husband-wife, parent-child, and your relationship with yourself and how work impacts that."

—Sarah

☎ "Be comfortable with your childcare situation and the demands of the job. I can't imagine having a rigid work schedule [with] three kids. Also, be honest with yourself when weighing the pros and cons (of the situation). Be sure you truly feel capable of handling the demands of family and home and work."

—Jane

☎ "First and foremost, consider the effect on your career. And by that I don't just mean that sometime-satisfaction of being employed but the effect on your earning power. You will need that someday. Can you keep a hand in? Can you freelance or work part-time? Can you pursue a significant project while you're home with your children? That isn't denigrating the enormous value of being a primary parent to children. It is, however, acknowledging the reality that the marketplace no longer will value you as highly."

—Amy

# Chapter 1

## Keeping track of yourself:
## Hold on to your identity.

*It is hard to fight an enemy who has outposts in your head.*
*Sally Kempton*

Janice grew up during the 1970s and '80s, when women were being taught that they could be whatever they wanted to be. It was the height of the women's movement; our role models fought so that our dreams could come true. Janice watched her dad and learned to judge success like he did—by money and power and status. It was nice having her Mom home after school, but she knew she wanted more for herself.

Women who grew up during this time wanted to succeed like their dads, often not recognizing that they might have a desire in the future to nurture like their Moms did. The fundamental conflict that Mothers today face is how to bridge the gap between their goal-oriented, ambitious, assertive individual needs and their desire to be a nurturer, the patient and kind Mother they long to be. In a society that encourages women to remain divided and choose between one path and the other, it is harder than ever to integrate the pieces.

Let's face it—we live in a world that defines us by what we do. Value is placed on success as the workplace defines it. Society directs the greatest respect to positions like doctors, directors, and CEOs. The value of women as Mothers is typically given lip service at best, except when it comes to the results of child-rearing; great value is placed on the end product, but rarely on the process in which women are so intricately involved. Despite the lack of support and respect Motherhood gets, Mothers are still blamed for most of the problems associated with their offspring.

As a result of the precarious position in which we find ourselves, it is so important that each of us assesses our own value by who we are and what our lives are about, not by some arbitrary definition of what society deems

11

valid. There are many aspects of our lives on which value cannot be placed, at least not in a monetary sense. It is too easy to allow tangible, work-related achievements and accomplishments to define us. However, in order to maintain a strong identity and sense of self, we must dig deeper. Each of us must separate who we are from what we do.

An outstanding metaphor for this process is presented by career counselor Shoya Zichy, in Elizabeth Perle McKenna's, *When Work Doesn't Work Anymore*. Ms. Zichy suggests that in the search for balance, you might think about rebuilding your life as a potter's hands construct a pot. She explains that, "It is keeping the pressure constant between them [the hands] that creates that pot. The outer hand is all the factors of genetics and intelligence and family support, expectations, education, and opportunities in life. If you have judged your whole life by how the outer hand is doing, the pot collapses on itself; that's what burnout is. The inner hand is the innate, inborn psychological type that dictates your preferences, what releases the most energy in you. That's the one we don't have a handle on...It's when you start to trust the inner hand that you regain balance and control."[1]

If you are employed, you may define yourself to a large extent by what you do: claims adjuster, pediatrician, librarian, retail clerk, entrepreneur. I encourage you to separate *who* you are from *what* you do, just like the potter. You may very well have confidence in yourself as an employee, but don't let yourself be satisfied with that. You are complex and multi-dimensional. What about your role as individual, as daughter, as Mother, friend, spiritual being, employee, partner, and volunteer? Define success in ways apart from your occupation. Though it can be difficult, keep an eye on your "inner hand." Identify your roles and look at your strengths in each. What do you most admire about you? What are you most proud of as a Mother, as a partner, as a friend? If you could start over, do you see yourself doing the same things you do now or taking a different path? Why? Can you make changes that lead you toward the path you thought you wanted?

If you are home with your children, searching for your meaning—your inner hand—can be a painful part of the transition from employment to home. In a social setting, the first question often asked after exchanging names is, "What do you do?" The employed Mother finds a comfort zone in that conversation. The Mother who stays home with her children may experience that throat-closing feeling of anxiety as she blurts, "I, uh, I used to...," or, "I do a little consulting." It is easy to get caught up in the roles of Mother and partner and lose yourself in the process.

The first months a woman is home with her children are typically filled with much angst, according to the women I spoke with. So much of who they are was wrapped up in what they did. They are no longer recognized for the great speech, the wonderful proposal, or the terrific grant, and most of the things they do accomplish are intangible anyway. Maybe your children are different, but I don't usually hear mine say, "Wow, Mom—thanks for emptying the dishwasher"; "Thanks for reading Pooh Bear again for the 19th time today"; "Thanks for playing hide-n-seek all day"; or, "Thanks for taking me to my baseball games the last 10 days straight."

Although gratifying in some ways, being home with children day in and day out can be a tremendously isolating experience for a Mother. The support system she once relied on may have been disrupted since her support needs have changed. Her partner may be very happy she's decided to stay home and wants to support her any way he can, but he cannot truly understand the emotions she's dealing with. Or, maybe he's not supportive at all. "Home Alone Syndrome," first described by Cindy Tolliver in *At Home Motherhood*, illustrates what many women experience as full-time at-home Mothers: They feel isolated and have little adult interaction. Tolliver suggests it is widespread enough to be considered an occupational hazard of at-home parenting.[2]

The result of "Home Alone Syndrome" is some level of depression that most but not all parents "outgrow" after a period ranging from a few months to a year when new coping skills and support are developed. It is important for stay-at-home Mothers to reach out, either by contact with a Mothers' group, with a friend or neighbor who is home with her children, with Internet chat groups or boards, or by some other means.

During this time of transition for the new Mother at home, defining multiple roles can again help in seeing value in what she does. Setting objectives for herself and accomplishing them gives a valuable sense of self-worth. Jan, in the midst of a 4-year leave of absence from her position as middle school principal, maintains her Franklin-Covey scheduling planner as she did each day at work. It helps her set goals in her various roles as spiritual being, Mother, partner, individual, volunteer, friend, daughter. Jan measures her success by her ability to follow through with her objectives. She has never felt the feelings of failure and desperation so common in women home with their children, and she attributes that to planning and scheduling.

Whether job-sharing, maintaining full-time employment, or being at home full-time, we must constantly search for what's important to us. If we keep perspective in each of our complex roles, we will stay on track with our personal goals in life. Take time to search. Find the time. Negotiate for time by asking your partner or a babysitter or a parent or a friend to relieve you. It is that important.

## MELODY'S STORY

At first when I stayed home, I felt that I wasn't pulling my weight to support our family. I felt I needed to accomplish 'things' every day to justify my staying home. If my husband came home from work and the house wasn't picked up and dinner wasn't ready, I felt like a total failure. Face it—you don't get much done when you're home with two kids under three years old. I've had to learn to measure a good day by a trip to the library, a fun morning doing puzzles, two loads of laundry done. For a while, I didn't always take a shower during the day or put make-up on. To feel good about myself, I know that I have to take pride in each success of my day, no matter how silly it may seem sometimes. I feel better about myself if I take a shower and look decent. It's easy when you're home to spiral down to a point where you don't feel good about yourself and you start to lose touch with friends. My husband and I have talked about how important it is that I have time for myself. It also helps a lot when he asks me about my day without judging its productivity.

Melody, Mother of two

Jeremy, age 2-1/2

Susie, age 18 months

*Read each "Point for reflection." Challenge yourself to answer the "tough" questions. Use these questions simply as a starting point; let your writing follow your thoughts. Take your time. And remember: Growth and change come slowly and are seldom easy.*

## POINTS FOR REFLECTION

How do you measure success?

**Consider**—Start with some things you may see as insignificant but you know they get done only because of you. Don't underestimate the effort it takes to accomplish these things. What terms can you relate to "success" besides money and power?

*I can't judge success by results because I don't have control of them regarding kids.*

*I feel good if I manage to balance the time spent on teaching kids, house, and my intellectual development. I also need to be part of people's life, be able to help them with advice & action.*

*need to do what God wants me to.*

Describe five moments in your life when you felt really good about who you are.

**Consider**—Perhaps it's a moment when you gave of yourself, a time you went out of your way for someone, a time of recognition.

1. I feel good every time I tell people that I have 3 kids
2. I felt good to org. lunches at Schreiber.
3. I felt good getting Bill & Stan through the line to the train
4. I felt good for being able to do hard gardening for 2 weeks
5. I feel good dressed up.

Name six qualities you *really* like about yourself.

**Consider**—Not your brown hair or long legs, but the important things inside.

1. I want to learn to love like God wants us to.
2. Responsible
3. Capable of hard work even hard physical labor
4. Sense of humor
5. Smart

What's valuable about you? Imagine you are sitting across from your best friend. Tell her (or him) the three things you like most about her. What three things would she say she likes best about you?

**Consider**—Do this exercise in person with a good friend.

## CARRIE'S STORY

I always knew that I'd keep my job after we had children. I love my job, and it's a part of me. I love how it makes me feel about myself. The hard part is trying to get everything done. Sometimes I don't feel like I'm a good Mom, a good employee, or a good wife. It's hard not to think I could do it all if only I worked a little harder. When I start feeling that way, I do what I call 'reality checks' where I take a close look at how hard I am on myself. Usually, I am expecting way too much from myself. When I pull back and remember to think about what's really important, everything goes better. I'm still learning to be gentle with myself. But I think it's one of the keys to being fulfilled as a woman and as a Mother.

Carrie, Mother of two

Troy, age 6

Amy, age 4

## POINTS FOR REFLECTION

First, write down the five highest priorities in your life. Over the next week, list everything you do for yourself and for your family. Now look at your personal calendar. Does your schedule reflect the priorities you listed?

**Consider**—What steps will you take in order to better honor your priorities?

1. Love God & my neighbors
2. Raise happy children/people
3. Cherish rel. with sean
4. Maintain family connections
5. Develop myself intellectusly

How will you go about setting clear boundaries?

**Consider**—From now on, when you're asked to do something (by your boss, partner, church, or other volunteer organization), don't answer on the spot. Maybe you'd say "I want to discuss this with my partner, " or, "I need a day or two to think about my calendar." Take time to think about whether that fits into your schedule and whether you have time to add to your "to do" list.

*Compare my priorities list with my weekly schedule.*

## JOANNE'S STORY

Before I had children and moved to Minnesota, I enjoyed a successful career as an engineer. I am home with my children full-time now, and it works for my family. But everyone I meet here knows me as my husband's wife and Joey, Kim, and Mark's Mom. Sometimes I want to jump up and down waving my arms saying, "I'm smart and capable. I used to be an engineer." I feel stereotyped. I feel like when people look at me they think I'm lazy, not so bright, and spoiled. It's wrong. I know a lot of really smart women, over-achieving women who decided to spend a few years at home with their children. I sometimes feel swallowed up in everyone else's stuff—I, me, I get lost somewhere. It's so hard. I never thought I'd have an identity crisis over this!

> JoAnne, Mother of three
>
> Joey, age 14
> Kim, age 11
> Mark, age 5

## POINTS FOR REFLECTION

List each of your roles. Describe the significance of each.

*Wife* → *maintain unity of me & Sean*
*share in Sean's life so he*
*is not lonely*

*Mother* → *mental & physical*
*wellbeing of my children*

*Family manager* → *house keeping*
*activity planning*
*issue presenter/researcher*
*project management*

*Daughter, sister, other* → *provide connection*
*help in need*

*Friend* → *provide help & support*
*maintain connection*

*Individual* → *spiritual development*
*intellectual development*

*Member of society/commu- nity* → *church vol. work*

> **Consider**—What do you do as a friend, sister, daughter, individual, spiritual being, partner, Mother to strengthen that relationship?

Choose two roles and define one goal for yourself in each role over the next week.

**Consider**—What will I realistically do in each of these roles? For example, as a sister, I will send pictures of the kids to John and send a birthday card to Mark.

wife - date Sean

friend - letter to Gretel

Mother - party for Tatiana

Can you see the connection between your value system and the life you're currently leading?

Yes, but I spend more time on less important things

## SALLY'S STORY

I worked as a researcher in a pharmaceutical lab for a long time before I decided to take a few years off to be with Anthony and David. I thought I was ready for it but quickly felt the isolation and loneliness I'd read about. The biggest thing for me, though, was that I felt like my world got smaller somehow, like my 'only' responsibility now was for my family. On one hand, that responsibility often feels overwhelming, but on the other hand, it felt too one-dimensional. Is that weird? It's not that what I did in the lab was so great or anything, but I felt like I was contributing to something bigger, I guess. At home, I didn't feel like I was making much of a difference. I spent a lot of time thinking about my purpose at this stage of my life. As my role at home evolved, I know now that I touch people in a lot of new ways. I'm a better friend because I have time to be a better friend. I'm on a great committee at church that has helped me develop a stronger spirituality. It took time and a lot of reflection, but I've learned so much about my real self.

Sally, Mother of two

Anthony, age 6
David, age 3

## POINTS FOR REFLECTION

If you could invite any five women to have lunch with you (dead or alive; famous or not) who would they be? Why? What values do they possess that you honor as well?

*Karen Armstrong - smart*
*Tracy - she has strong & clear values*
*Tracy's Mom - how she brought up such nice children & strong family*
*Jason's Mom - same*
*Gail - persevere; acceptance*

What are your greatest gifts? List at least five.

**Consider**—Describe how you will begin to better use one of those gifts this week.

Describe how you will reframe the idea that raising a family means "I'm just home with my kids."

**Consider**—Raising a family is a valid, valuable undertaking. What advice would you give to a friend who said to you, "I'm just home with my kids?"

## ENDNOTES

[1] McKenna, Elizabeth Perle. *When Work Doesn't Work Anymore: Women, Work, And Identity*, pages 170-171.

[2] Tolliver, Cindy. *At-Home Motherhood: Making It Work for You*, pages 129-144.

## ADDITIONAL RESOURCES

### Books

*Surrendering to Motherhood: Losing Your Mind, Finding Your Soul*, by Iris Krasnow
*Motherhood At The Crossroads: Meeting the Challenge of a Changing Role*, by Sue Lanci Villani

### Websites

www.NMHA.org
National Mental Health Association (800) 969-NMHA
A non-profit organization addressing all areas of mental health, including depression

www.MOPS.org
Mothers of Preschoolers
An international support group with a Christian focus

www.Momsclub.org
The Moms Club
A unique women's organization designed for at-home Mothers

www.mothersandmore.org
Mothers & More (formerly FEMALE)
A support and advocacy network for sequencing women

www.mochaMoms.org
Mocha Moms
A support group for women of color who have chosen not to work full-time outside the home

www.mah.org
Mothers at home

# Chapter 2

## Expectations:
## Turn them off.

*You have to get strong enough to let your values override
the values of the culture and the values of the corporation.*

Anna Quindlen

"Damned if I do and damned if I don't." That's how Carol describes today's cultural attitudes toward women and employment. If she works outside the home she's judged as selfish and doesn't care enough about her children. If she stays home with her children, she's called lazy and too involved in their lives. Current research sends contradicting messages about children and development and childcare as well. Some recommend the Mother or father should be with the child for at least the first three years of life. Others say that quality childcare typically stimulates children's brains better than a home environment. Still others advocate that a child raised in childcare is more self-sufficient or that a child with a stay-at-home parent has stronger bonds with his family. It is more art than science when it comes to family-work issues.

The women's movement afforded women the opportunity to be whatever we want to be. We learned to work hard and to stay focused on our goals. We learned to measure our value by our contributions to the workplace. Our identity arose from what we did. Then we had children. We thought we could have it all—a profession and all that came with it, then have a partner and children as well. We not only thought we COULD do it all, we received overt and covert messages that we *should* do it all.

There is no cultural norm for women as Mothers to follow as this new millennium dawns. On one hand, it feels good because we are making the rules. The down side is that during this time of Mother-anarchy, there is no tried and true history to rely on. The message was clear to our Mothers.

They stayed home with their children and there were few exceptions. In the 80s, women found employment and stayed employed, for the most part. And now, at a time when women were raised to do whatever it is they want, those choices get so confusing we're often not sure what we want. Or should want. And whatever choice we finally make, we are condemned by part of society for making the "wrong decision." The Mommy wars may be over, but the ashes continue to smolder.

Regardless of employment status, the "myth of the ideal Mother" lives on in all of us. You know her. She's that fairy tale-like-Mother who always seems to have a voice in our lives. Whether we're home with children full-time, employed part-time or full-time, telecommute or job share, she continues to be a particularly destructive role model despite the rumors that SuperMom is dead. As a Mother and a woman, we strive to attain the homemaking skills of Martha Stewart, the pediatric and childraising expertise of T. Berry Brazelton, and the work accomplishments of Madeleine Albright. The problem is that "there's too much emphasis on the idea that there's only one acceptable model of child and one acceptable model of Mom when, in fact, there are 99 million" as maintained by Ann Weinstein, director of a San Francisco-based resource center for parents.[1]

In my interviews, I asked women about their image of the "ideal Mother." See if any of these sound familiar:
- She is endlessly patient with her children despite the three hours of sleep she got the night before.
- She looks incredible—perfect makeup, no peanut butter or formula stains.
- Her children get perfect grades.
- She exercises faithfully every day before the kids wake up.
- Her children are always perfectly behaved in public.
- She works full-time and her children don't torture her for it when she picks them up at childcare.
- After picking the kids up from childcare, she leisurely drives home after work and makes a nice dinner while her young children happily and quietly play close by.
- Dinnertime is always calm and full of happy news.

- The house is always organized and clean.
- The children go to bed without a fight and without once coming out of their room.
- She and her partner contentedly spend time talking about their days after the children are in bed.
- She and her partner fall asleep in each other's arms each night after mutually satisfying sex.

You may have seen this woman at June Cleaver's house, but not in the homes of the women with whom I spoke. Admittedly outlandish, we as women and Mothers still tend to gauge ourselves by this unrealistic measuring stick. The Ghost of June lives on.

Most of the women I interviewed went through a period after the birth or adoption of a child when they donned SuperMom garb. Whether they were proving it to themselves, their partner, their corporation, or their Mother, the stakes were high and they felt the need to be successful on all fronts. Then came the realization that SuperMom doesn't exist—the understanding that each of us makes sacrifices to balance the whole. Nanci Olesen, artist, actor, and radio show host, put it like this, "That first year after I had Henry, I had a teaching position 70 miles away from home. I started a radio show, MOM-bo, for which I stayed up late at night preparing. I worked at a bookstore, creating window displays. I performed at the "Heart of the Beast" Christmas show, I planned a May Day celebration, I was in a Mom's group, I aired a piece on Minnesota Public Radio on 'Moms at home, Moms at work.'"

When I asked Nanci what finally happened when she stopped, she said "There was tiredness and some shock about how tired I was and some shock about how much I liked being a Mom. That whole upheaval led to inventing MOM-bo, my current radio show about Mothering. Now, I'm more directed. I'm more interested in myself and in taking care of myself and in being by myself. It's not as important to me to go out and help everyone else. I respect myself more."

The expectations imposed upon us range from subtle to overt. The force each influence exerts over us is individual. It's hazy where outside expectations end and our own beliefs and realistic expectations of ourselves begin. The diagram below describes the many places expectations come from:

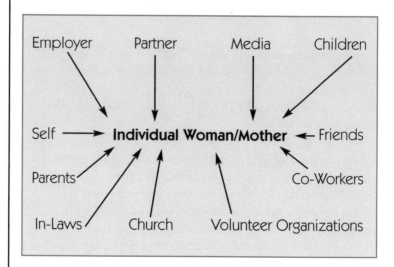

Each of us must separate our own self from the outside messages we constantly receive telling us what kind of person we should be and what sort of choices we should make regarding our lives, our families, our careers. We cannot control what those external influences think or say. We can control who we are, what we do with our lives, what sort of model we put forth for others to see and for our children to see.

To get a clearer picture of your own values independent of external influences, follow this three-step process. It will help you to start seeing or to remember what is most important to you.

1. **Identify the influences that most affect you.**
   Maybe it's the culture of your workplace. Or your partner. Perhaps it's your stay-at-home friends who always have something to say about your work schedule. Determine whether or not each influence is significant enough to address (if it's really troubling you, it's big enough to address). *Mother, grandfather*

*Tracy - advice*
*Mother - better*

2. **Take time to reflect on each major influence and address the issue in an appropriate way.**
   Could you talk to your Mother, your employer, your friend? Why is it so important for you to satisfy that influence? For example, if your Mother always thought you should stay home with your children and you've decided to stay employed but feel guilty when you talk to her, what can you do about that? Can you talk to her about how you feel? If not, you must find a way to resolve it in your heart. As you confront each expectation, cross it off your diagram.

3. **Look at what's left.**
   You. What do you look like? What's in your heart? What do you miss about your life before children? What do you love about your life with children? Have you left any of your dreams behind? Why? Now, be deliberate about how you begin to filter those influences.

*Спросить маму, почему она всё время толкает*

*Дед Серёй – resolve in my heart.*

*I do not miss anything in my life before children. They give me fulfillment and freedom to do whatever I want. Dreams? I never had any. Ambition? Yes. Но это не такая большая ценность. Их не можно боле всеуросить*

*Важно ли что то решаешь, а как решаешь, ни к чему вообще, ни к плохому ... минуте жизни.*

*как была ... Ты к чему не привыкоровался а пробовался каждой ши к хорошему а пробовался каждой минуте жизни.*

## CONNIE'S STORY

I managed to "do it all" for quite some time and everyone around me marveled at how I ever did it. I had two children, worked 55 hours a week, I exercised regularly, cooked meals, and kept a clean house. Then everything changed. My husband, children, and I went on a two-week vacation a while back. It was then that I realized it. Even though to the outside world I was doing it all, I didn't feel like I did any of it the way I really wanted to. I wanted to spend more time with Spencer and Carrie, yet if I did, my work suffered. Instead of making mental notes and 'promising' not to get out of control again once I got back to work, my husband and I talked about it and followed through on some major changes that would affect our family in a positive way. I downsized my job, lessened how much the children were in after school care, and lowered my expectations of myself. I feel so liberated. I'm happier, more in balance—and so is the rest of my family.

Connie, Mother of two
Spencer, age 9
Carrie, age 7

*Read each "Point for reflection." Challenge yourself to answer the "tough" questions. Use these questions simply as a starting point; let your writing follow your thoughts. Take your time. And remember: Growth and change come slowly and are seldom easy.*

## POINTS FOR REFLECTION

**Consider**—This could be time alone or with your partner, but in a quiet place which lends itself to reflection.
How will you do this?
Are you going to write?
Talk to someone?
When—specifically?
Plan it now.

Can you find time to get away to reflect on your priorities and the pace of your life?

*Trip to Tracy in June.*
*Write.*
*Trip to the farm.*
*Write*
*Letter to mother.*
*Write.*

After taking time away from your everyday life, do you regularly "promise" to keep your life in better perspective and to maintain a better sense of balance?

*By the time Sophia goes to school I want to have a /study/research plan to (intensive) determine my interests and plans*
*What is different? I do not do this for my Mom and grandfather*

> **Consider**—How will this time be different? Be specific.

What is it that drives you to the pace you are living?

*I am jogging - no to nor from. I have a good time.*

> **Consider**—Are you running to something or away from something?

## JOYCE'S STORY

Sometimes I think that by choosing to stay home with my children I've let everyone down. I feel like I've let my Dad down—we always dreamed together of what I'd 'do with my life.' Plus he paid my college and graduate school tuition. I've let society down because there's so little support for women like me. I often feel like I've let all women down. The women's movement was so important for women's rights and I appreciate what women before me have done. I have two undergraduate degrees and a master's degree. The last thing I imagined is that I would have a child, let alone want to stay home with her. So, now I can't help but feel that I've turned my back. I have to keep reminding myself that the women's movement was all about choices—it's about giving women opportunities within which to make their own best decision. Isn't it?

Joyce, Mother of one
Kim, age 2-1/2

## POINTS FOR REFLECTION

Identify the influences (identified on page 28) that most affect you. Mother , grandfather

Why do you care what those influences really think? Really—WHY?

I want them to think good about me

What's your first step to take some of the pressure off?

*I can talk to my Mom*

> **Consider**—Can you talk to any of those influences?

Are you still content with your decision to be home full-time with your child(ren)?

*Yes*

> **Consider**—Perhaps it is time to reconsider work options.

## BETHANY'S STORY

Why do I feel so much pressure to have everything RIGHT? If my friends and colleagues knew how "not right" I feel most of the time, they'd die! Everyone thinks I have it so together, but the truth is, I can't do it anymore! It's just not working for anyone, least of all me. I cannot find time to work out every day, make dinner, keep the kids happy and have a tidy house. OK, I finally admit it. I can't meet everyone's expectations. My Mom, who lives about three hours away, called yesterday to tell us that there's a birthday party for one of my nephews on Sunday. She totally expects us to be there! Joe has soccer and Martie has piano lessons. How am I going to do this? Mark's going to kill me when he hears. We were just planning to hang out at home this weekend. Why do I always feel like I have to do these things I really don't want to do?

Bethany, Mother of two

Joe, age 12
Martie, age 7

## POINTS FOR REFLECTION

Do you have a friend, work peer, family member who just seems to have it all together?

**Consider**—Talk to her about it. Chances are, she struggles too. You may get some good tips from her.

*Tracy*
*ask her about*
*her expectations of herself*

Why do you want everyone to think you always are in control and have your act together?

*I want to be liked and admired ?*

> **Consider**—How would others react to know that sometimes you're not *so* together?

Circle the values below that are most important to you.

| | | | |
|---|---|---|---|
| Integrity | Trust | Flexibility | Authenticity |
| Courage | Health | Respect | Fun |
| Humor | Productivity | Justice | Acceptance |
| Vitality | Recognition | Risk-taking | Diversity |
| Focus | Harmony | Honesty | Adventure |
| (Growth) | (Compassion) | (Connection with God) | Free-spirit |

Are you honoring the values most important to you?

*No*

> **Consider**—Does your life reflect that?

35

## DONNA'S STORY

About two years ago, I downsized my position to part-time. It was a hard decision because I really like my job. I just felt this tug to be with my family more. From a family stand-point, I couldn't be much happier—I finally feel like I can spend real time with my children. My husband, Tim, and I have a little breathing room. That's not the problem. The problem is that since I went to part-time, everyone else seems to feel like they can have a piece of me, too. Like Maggie, Steven, and Alicia's school. They call all the time looking for volunteers. Our church has asked me to partici-pate in three new project teams; my Mother-in-law thinks we should be able to visit at least once a week; and Tim thinks I should be able to fit all the errands, housework and cooking in my "spare time." Plus, I feel like I have the same workload at the office—just less time to do it. This is crazy. Time for me STILL doesn't fit into the equation!

Donna, Mother of three

Maggie, age 13
Steven, age 11
Alicia, age 7

## POINTS FOR REFLECTION

How will you create clear boundaries for yourself?

**Consider**—Protect the time you worked so hard to create. Say yes when you can; say no when you must.

Identify the influences that most affect you (from page 28).

What is it about those influences that make it difficult to say "no"?

What two small changes can you make in your life to reflect the lifestyle you are searching for?

> **Consider**—Be mindful of why you chose to spend more time with your family. For example, talk to your partner who thinks you should assume all household tasks.

Make time for yourself. Schedule it. Don't cancel.

What can I do for myself?

> **Consider**—Schedule time and plan what you will do with that time. Negotiate with a friend or your partner to keep this time sacred.

# ENDNOTES

[1] Villani, Sue Lanci. *Motherhood at the Crossroads: Meeting the Challenge of a Changing Role*, page 130.

# ADDITIONAL RESOURCES

## Books

*The Mother Dance*, by Harriet Lerner, Ph.D.
*Good Enough Mothers: Changing Expectations of Ourselves*, by Melinda M. Marshall.

## Websites

www.ivillage.com
> Consists of more than 15 channels, including career, health and wellness, family, and money. Also provides links to 10 women's magazine sites, including *Good Housekeeping*, *Redbook*, and *Town and Country*.

www.kfai.org
> Radio station that is home to MOM-bo, a show for women with an attitude.

# Chapter **3**

## Collaborative couple:
## Your relationship is key.

*"All marriages are happy. It's trying to live together
afterwards that causes all the problems."*

*Shelley Winters*

Kristine believed in her heart of hearts that she'd be different. Her friends, her family—everyone told her how her life would change after her baby was born. At 34, she had a successful career and a great marriage to her high-school sweetheart, Matt. When their son Josh finally arrived, Kristine quickly realized that "everyone" had been right. Everything was different. Kristine's lifestyle was changing in ways unimaginable to her before. She watched her feelings about work change; her relationship with Matt changed; her very identity was different.

Most people say it is easier to be equal partners in a relationship before there are children. In fact, most divorce occurs during child-rearing years, according to Betty Carter, M.S.W., family counselor and author of *Love, Honor & Negotiate.* When a child is born and a woman begins to consider work options, her issues become very different from her partner's. It is a time when growing apart is easy for couples. "Their world isn't organized to allow them to remain equal," Carter says.[1] Add sleep deprivation and inadequate time for each other, and the marriage can fall apart.

The women I interviewed frequently complained about how a once-equal partnership became hopelessly lopsided after the adoption or birth of a child. As a new Mom, you wonder how it happened. Partners must be deliberate in their attempt to maintain a sense of equilibrium at this point or the woman will likely find herself doing two-thirds of the housework, performing most of the child care, and losing momentum in her job.

One of the most interesting findings from my interviews was that, even in homes where both partners held professional full-time positions, women remained the core and chief executive officer at home. She's the one who fills out the permission slips and volunteers in the classroom; she writes the check for hot lunch; she shops for the kids' clothes and stays home when they're sick. The work pendulum swings in the direction of the Mother, to be sure.

Emotionally, partners struggle with how to support one another at a time when they can no longer easily identify with what the other is experiencing. For the most part, men count on a linear path from graduation to retirement. Though they will probably change employer and position, they typically remain employed full-time whether single or married, whether childless or the father of three. When a woman chooses the path of marriage and Motherhood, on the other hand, the road splits, narrows, and curves on countless occasions, providing many distractions throughout her years of raising children.

Fortunately Kristine, our bewildered Mother from the beginning of the chapter, had a number of options as she turned to her husband, Dick, for his thoughts. Kristine's manager at work told her (with much apprehension) that she could telecommute two days each week. Financially a stretch, they could make it on one income, so staying home with Josh was a second option. Or, she could continue to work full-time as she had always done. Dick insisted that they would work it out together. They talked about how they could each define work differently. They wondered if they could design their jobs so that Josh didn't spend many hours each week in childcare and that they would share his care. Maybe Dick could work his hours differently on the days Kristine worked part-time.

These discussions are grueling. But here's where Kristine was totally right—she knew they had to discuss and negotiate their work and family choices and the effects her decisions would have on Dick. Kristine did not assume that Dick would know what she was thinking through some sort of telepathic communication. She initiated the tough conversations about childcare and parenting. This couple is on the right road.

If we expect the workplace to change, each of us is responsible for asking the tough questions: How will my partner and I redefine how we do work? Where can we physically get our work done? How can we continue to be valued employees while feeling like instrumental parts of our child's life?

The ThirdPath Institute, a non-profit organization dedicated to helping people redesign work to create time for other life priorities, introduced the concept of Shared Care. Shared Care teaches couples about a new model of balancing work and family by redesigning work to shared responsibilities between work and family.

Most couples aren't as far along in the discussions as Shared Care dreams or as Dick and Kristine are. Dick knows the kind of support he will need to offer his family. As women, we must understand what our partners mean when they say they "support" us. For example, does it mean:

- You can tell him when you've had a lousy day and he'll reassure you, telling you that things will be better tomorrow?
- He will take the kids to childcare on Tuesdays and Thursdays?
- The two of you will discuss calendars each Sunday for the upcoming week and decide who can drive to childcare, take the kids to soccer, make (or pick up) dinner, etc.?
- You can negotiate who stays home when one of the children is sick?
- He will tell you he supports you but will not participate in any child-related issues?
- You share household duties like laundry, cleaning, cooking, grocery shopping?
- You share responsibility for who puts the kids to bed, reads to them, helps them with their homework?

If you renegotiate what you need for support from your partner, I caution you that you will need to change the way you support your partner, too. If we want and expect our partners to participate in maintaining the house and raising good kids, we must also support them in ways that are meaningful to them. Value their ways of doing things for what they are—not right or wrong but simply different from your way. Here's what I've learned about support through my interviews, research, and personal experience:

- Don't undermine your partner's contributions to the children, to the household, or to you. As hard as it may be to give up control of the traditional domain for women, it is essential. Your partner won't cook like you, grocery shop like you, or put the kids to bed like you. But he will still, in all likelihood, do it "right." As we encourage our mates to participate, we must let them do it their way—without sarcasm, nagging, or telling them a better way!
- Ask him about the tasks he wants to accomplish over a weekend and help him get them done.
- Don't hand him a list of things to get done (unless he likes it that way); discuss and negotiate house projects and who will complete what tasks when.
- Make love to your partner frequently. Sometimes he wants it and you don't. But you will probably find it's nice for both of you; he's satisfied; he may hold you all night and pour you coffee in the morning.

You know those same people who told you that your life would change overnight when you had a baby no doubt also told you that marriage is a lot of work? Once again, they were right. Rick and I didn't feel like we worked at our marriage until C.J. was born. We agreed on most everything and if we didn't, it didn't really matter much. Marriage after children is a lot of work. But there are ways to stay connected with your partner. Search for those ways. Follow through. If none of the following ideas feels right, find others or you may find yourself in the 50% of the marriages that don't survive.

**Set aside time each day to catch up with each other.**
Get up and have a cup of coffee together before the kids are up and one or both of you leave for work; put your kids to bed early enough in the evening so that you have time to talk, uninterrupted; or, if your kids are a bit older (my kids understood by the time they were three or so), have a short time in the evening when they cannot interrupt the two of you.

**Discuss the logistics of your day.**
Who is picking up the kids? Who is driving them to the birthday party? Who is making (or picking up) dinner?

**Schedule periodic dates.**
Maybe it's weekly, maybe it's monthly. Do something both of you enjoy apart from your children.

**Turn off the TV at night and read the paper, flip through a magazine, or do a puzzle together.**
Just be together.

**Send e-mail cards, snail mail cards, or love letters to his office.**

**Schedule dates in your bedroom after the kids are asleep.**
Listen to music, share a glass of wine, read the newspaper together. This is a wonderful rendezvous, particularly if you leave an invitation somewhere for him to see.

**Call him during the day to tell him that you love him.**
That's it, nothing else.

Children do best when they have an involved Mother and father. Keep your marriage a priority. For you. For your partner. For your children.

## KAREN'S STORY

Before we had our children, John and I were truly partners. We both worked about 60 hours a week with comparable salaries, but when we were together, we were a team. We did errands together; we shared household responsibilities pretty equally. Naturally, I thought when we brought Abraham back from Russia, we would share the responsibilities he brought with him as well. Something happened, though—I don't quite understand it. I immediately became his primary care-giver—primary bather, feeder, diaper changer. I'm the one it seems who was somehow designated to take him to the doctor, the one to get up with him at night. When I went back to work, I was the one taking him to childcare and picking him up. After months of harboring a fair amount of anger about all this, we had a lot of discussions about how we would be partners. It's not perfect, but it's better. Negotiating who is going to do what for a week at a time is now an on-going discussion. I know I'll always be the household manager, but that's OK because my needs are getting met, too.

Karen, Mother of one

Abraham, age 19 months

*Read each "Point for reflection." Challenge yourself to answer the "tough" questions. Use these questions simply as a starting point; let your writing follow your thoughts. Take your time. And remember: Growth and change come slowly and are seldom easy.*

## POINTS FOR REFLECTION

What does "support" mean to you? How does your partner define it? *If Sean:*

*1. Truly curious about my days*
*2. Admits that he does not know what it means to be a stay-home Mom and he would not judge.*
*3. Would give me time alone*

**Consider**—Most partners are supportive in an emotional sense—they want each other to be happy. It is important to discuss what you mean in an everyday, how-it-affects-your-partner's-life, sense.

Are you well-supported? In a perfect world, what would support mean? What do you suppose it would mean to your partner?

*To support Sean means:*
*1. Provide him with welcoming comf. home environment*
*2. Appreciate his efforts no matter the results.*
*3. Let him play*

**Consider**—Are your ideas realistic?

How will you go about re-negotiating your roles?

**Consider**—Plan how you're going to discuss these issues with your partner. Will it be on a date? Early on a Saturday morning? After the kids go to bed one night?

For one week, you and your partner record all home and child-related activities. Compare after one week. Does the workload feel fair?

**Consider**—Begin talking about how to make workloads more equitable. No sarcasm, no competitions, please.

Many collaborative couples plan driving schedules, dinner schedules, and social schedules each Sunday—before each workweek begins.

**Consider**—Would this work for you?

## MARY'S STORY

I just miss him. Plain and simple. We used to travel, go to fun restaurants, laugh and play. Three children later, I feel like we barely keep our heads above water. We look at each other after the kids are in bed and smile with the knowing exhausted look that's become way too familiar. We love each other, I know that. And we have a great family. I just miss being alone with my best friend.

Mary, Mother of three

Susan, age 8
Freddie, age 4
Charlie, age 18 months

## POINTS FOR REFLECTION

What are the things you most enjoyed doing together before you had children? What were your partner's favorite things? Which could you occasionally plan into your life now?

*Travelling, hiking, camping dancing, playing board games, chess*

**Consider**—Could you hire a babysitter or trade babysitting time with a friend so that you could do some of those activities?

How will you carve out 20 minutes of uninterrupted time together into each day to catch up?

**Consider**—Try before your children are up, after dinner each night, after the kids are in bed.

47

What could you request of your partner to feel closer during this particularly exhausting phase of parenting?

**Consider**—He can't read your mind.

*We should talk eye-to-eye regularly.*

How does love show up in your life today? How can you bring more brightness to your life?

How will you show your partner that you're thinking of him and you want him to know how special he is to you?

**Consider**—E-mail cards, a phone call, a massage, candles with dinner.

## CINDY'S STORY

Gary finally said he'd help. I was so happy—we were moving toward an equal partnership for the first time since Macalah and Sheila were born. So one Sunday night, we talked about who would do what for the next week—taking the kids to their practices and lessons, grocery shopping, putting the kids to bed, cleaning, picking up or cooking dinner—you know the routine. I wanted this to work, so I told him he could pick what he thought he could handle first. (Before this, I'd done everything, so even if he just chose one thing it would help.) He said he'd do the grocery shopping and put the kids to bed on Monday, Thursday, and Friday night. Super, we agreed. He took the running grocery list off of the refrigerator. He came back with half of the wrong brands and twice as much as I usually buy. I was so mad, I just lit into him. I said, 'We've been married for 14 years and you don't know what brand of jelly I buy???' It turned into a huge fight. Putting the kids to bed was no better. They were up there playing and laughing until bedtimes came. They went to sleep pretty much when they were supposed to, but it was so LOUD compared to how I do it. When I brought it up to him, we started fighting again. He said that's why he doesn't help me—I always yell at him for how he does it.

Cindy, Mother of two
Macalah, age 10
Sheila, age 9

## POINTS FOR REFLECTION

If your partner agrees to handle some of the things you've done in the past, those things won't be done the way you did them. Ask yourself, "Does it really matter?"

*No*

**Consider**—The grocery shopping was done, the kids were asleep more-or-less when they were supposed to be. He did those things *differently*, not wrong.

How important is your standard? Is there only one right way (your way) to do a particular task?

*No*

**Consider**—Why is it important to do it your way? Wouldn't it benefit the kids to see new ways of getting the same result?

How do you feel when your partner pitches in? Evaluate why you feel the need to assert power in a historically female domain (the house).

**Consider**—You can continue to do it all yourself or you can accept that there's more than one way to vacuum the living room.

## CAROL'S STORY

My decision to stay home with Ellie and Olivia was gut-wrenching. When I finally made the break, I didn't look back and it's going pretty well. While I was working, we had a cleaning service and Mark and I shared most everything else when it came to running the house. The second I was home full-time, though, I found myself suddenly in charge of everything. I'm not staying home to keep the house sparkly or get all the errands done myself or assume 100% responsibility of the kids. I wanted to be with the kids, not be the maid. I'm happy to shoulder more of the home-related responsibilities, but this is ridiculous.

Carol, Mother of two

Ellie, age 7

Olivia, age 4

## POINTS FOR REFLECTION

What does it mean to be home with the kids?

**Consider**—What does it feel like to be there? What does it look like? What are your expectations and the expectations of those around you?

What specific home and child-related responsibilities do you consider yours? List them.

*Child: - classes*
*- teaching*
*- health*
*- social contacts*

*Home: cleaning*
*3 / cooking*
*pros shopping*
*other shopping*
*decorating*

**Consider these examples**—"I'm the one who will take Gina to gymnastics Tuesdays at 10:00 a.m."; "I'll do the grocery shopping with the kids,"; "I'll do the breakfast and lunch dishes."

What specific home and child-related responsibilities do you consider your partner's? What would you like to see your partner take on?

*- taking kids to school*
*- !*

*- teaching*

How will you begin negotiating the middle ground?

**Consider**—Not in the heat of argument, I hope. Set up some time when you will not be interrupted to begin clearly discussing your goals, what you expect from yourself, where you think your partner could step in.

## ENDNOTES

[1] Carter, Betty, M.S.W. *Love, Honor & Negotiate: Building Partnerships that Last A Lifetime*, page 15.

## ADDITIONAL RESOURCES

### *Books*

*Chore Wars*, by Jim Thornton
*Work and Family—Allies or Enemies*, by Stewart D. Friedman and
    Jeffrey H. Greenhaus
*And What Do You Do?: When Women Choose to Stay Home*, by Loretta
    Kaufman and Mary Quigley
*When Mothers Work: Loving Our Children Without Sacrificing Ourselves*, by
    Joan K. Peters
*She Works He Works: How Two-Income Families Are Happier, Healthier, and
    Better Off*, by Rosalind C. Barnett & Caryl Rivers
*It's Not the Glass Ceiling, It's the Sticky Floor and Other Things Our Daughters
    Should Know About Marriage, Work, and Motherhood*, by Karen
    Engberg, M.D.

### *Websites*

www.thirdpath.org
    The ThirdPath Institute
    A non-profit organization dedicated to helping people
    redesign work to create time for other life priorities

# Chapter 4

## Your need for financial independence: Shift in the balance of power?

*"Given that the majority of women want to work, that careers provide much more than money—self-esteem, expression, independence, and identity—it looks like women are deadlocked between two value systems whose conflicts create stress and breakdown. It is very hard to learn how to revalue things in our lives that had no value before."*

*Elizabeth Perle McKenna*

"Wow, I didn't expect this," Jane said. Until six weeks ago, this Mother of two had capably supported herself financially. "Deciding to stay home for a few years with our children was a big decision. I knew our spending habits would have to adjust dramatically, and I was prepared for that. I've been totally blindsided, though, by all this other stuff I can't seem to stop thinking about:

- Ah, I shouldn't have quit.
- I feel like I'm John's servant—I pick up his dry cleaning, do all the shopping, the dishes, cooking—everything! He thinks I have all this time now and isn't that part of my job?
- And my friend Dori was right—it is weird spending his—er, ours—oh, whoever's money…
- And, oh geez—if we ever got divorced, what would I do?"

Financial independence is a heated topic in the world for women today. The women's movement fought for it. Women in the paid workforce keep the fight alive in the equal-pay-for-equal-work battleground. As women, we are—and should be—proud of our accomplishments on this front. At the same time, when a woman chooses to step out of full-time employment for a period of time, the issue seems to grow three heads and four tails!

The implications of interrupting a career are far more complex than the physical loss of income. Many women I spoke with say that's actually the easy part. There are three other key issues that tend to be even more challenging. There are emotional concerns, like the feeling you're spending someone else's money. There are "balance of power" considerations—the question of who's in charge? Finally, there are personal finance concerns. What happens in the event that your marriage is one of the 50% that fail?

## LOSS OF INCOME

Loss of income may be the easiest of the four issues to face because you see it coming. The loss isn't easy, but you plan. You anticipate. I interviewed women whose families live on one income of $35,000-$40,000. Each of these women made it a priority to be home with her young children and they (as a family) made tremendous sacrifices to make that happen. Forgoing the purchase of a house, living with one car instead of two—these are realities in many families in order to have a parent at home.

There are a number of books and articles written on the topic of whether it's financially worthwhile for the partner (typically the woman) to work, based on her salary, child-care, and the indirect costs of her employment—if she's working solely for financial benefit. In Linda Kelley's book, *Two Incomes and Still Broke*, she explains that "It's risky to automatically assume another income will balance the books or provide the wherewithal for a better life. For most families there are monetary benefits, although not usually as many as expected, if both partners work outside the home. For others, the effort is wasted in a flow of job expenses that devour the second income and leave nothing but a bewildered and angry couple arguing over where the extra money went...."[1]

Can your family make it on one salary? Use the following simple form (from the book, *Staying Home: From Full-time Professional to Full-time Parent*) to calculate your real earnings after expenses.

| Income | Direct Expenses | | Real Earnings |
|---|---|---|---|
| | Taxes & benefits contributions | | |
| NOTE: your income amount should include salary plus any commissions and any 401K matching funds | Child care | | |
| | Household help | | |
| | Work-related clothing | | |
| | Meals out | | |
| | Professional expenses | | |
| | Transportation | | |
| | Totals: | | |
| Calculate | Reset | | |

INCOME – DIRECT EXPENSES = REAL EARNINGS

*Copyright 1999 by Darcie Sanders and Martha Bullen*[2]

## EMOTIONAL CONCERNS

The emotions that surround one's perception of money are significant. Since we were small children, we've been taught to define success by what we do and how much we make. Elizabeth Perle McKenna, author of *When Work Doesn't Work Anymore*, surveyed women about their views on money. The results were fascinating: Eighty percent said that money was critical to their sense of independence. Two-thirds felt judged by how much money they made, and more than two-thirds reported that money was important to their sense of well-being.[3]

Yet when McKenna asked them what they want out of their lives, the top four responses were non-materialistic: caring, connection, more time, and yes—of course—weight loss. Given the emphasis placed on the power and perception of wealth, is it any wonder that women who stay home with their children feel insecure about spending "someone else's money"?

## BALANCE OF POWER

Feminist Lillian Rubin once said, "Economic dependency brings emotional dependency—it's almost inevitable." Here's where it's important for women to learn to re-define success, or emotional dependence may indeed be inevitable. Through the first year or so at home with my oldest, I struggled intensely over this. I spent a lot of time reflecting, journaling, and talking to other women. After six years home with my children practically full-time, I now know the value I bring to the table, and I'm strong and clear about it. I bring stability, strong values, and predictability to a family where the bread-winner is away from home more than 100 nights each year. I am the core, the nucleus to three children whose foundation I am helping to build. Women who spend most of their time at home must be clear about their roles. They may not make direct deposits into the bank, but they do make direct deposits into the lives of each member of the family each day. If they don't value their role and equalize the balance of power in the relationship with their partner, they shouldn't be surprised when they feel and are treated like they're financially dependent.

## PERSONAL FINANCE

Legitimately, there is real concern on the part of women about the financial repercussions should their marriage dissolve. The fear of divorce is strong enough in a number of women I interviewed that they would not consider leaving the job market altogether. "My Mom and dad got divorced and my Mom was out of luck," Tammy told me; "she'd never really worked before. My dad didn't give us much help financially, and it was horribly humiliating for her. I will never put my children or myself in a position like that. EVER." Amy Gage, senior editor *of Minneapolis-St.Paul Magazine*, is so emphatic about the subject that she goes so far as to say that it's irresponsible for Mothers to set themselves up for financial failure by stepping out of the workplace altogether.

"To protect yourself, remember that 'knowledge is power,'" says Cindy Bottleson, who has 19 years of experience as a financial planner for American Express Financial Services. "Maintain awareness and participation in household budget and investment decision-making." She also encourages taking advantage of IRAs and Roth IRAs for non-wage earning spouses and employing a financial advisor and estate-planning attorney, as needed.

In spite of the difficulty for stay-at-home Moms to land on their feet in the case of divorce, there is a trend toward divorced women's recouping some percentage of their husbands' salaries in a divorce settlement. A woman who is the primary caretaker and core of her family and who supports her husband in the career that supports the family may be able to take credit for some level of his success. Take the story of Lorna and Gary Wendt. In 1998, they divorced after 32 years of marriage. Lorna spent many years as a corporate wife supporting Gary in his rise to become CEO of General Electric Capital Corporation. She concluded that she was therefore half-responsible for his tremendous success. She sued him for half of his worth—$100 million. Lorna was awarded $20 million by a judge in Connecticut.

As frightening as it may be to consider the ramifications of divorce for a woman who is not in the job market, most have something our Mothers did not—job experience. Most have established themselves in a career or have significant job experience. They feel that if their marriage fell apart, they have marketable skills. That's one of the benefits of sequencing. ("Sequencing" is a word coined by Arlene Cardozo in her book of the same name to define a woman who first establishes a career, then leaves full-time work while her children are young, and then incorporates a career back into her life.) As Linda put it, "I know that if the floor fell out from under me, I'd land on my feet. I'm not naïve. I've done it before; I can do it again. I know I can take care of myself."

## NANCY'S STORY

I decided to stay home full-time with my children after my second, Jodi, was born. I had always worked since I was 16. I'd supported myself for years. I felt good about that. I knew it would be a challenge for me to be without an income. It felt really awkward at first. At first, I felt like the money was *his* and that I was borrowing it or worse, taking it. My partner fully supports this decision to stay home and really sees the money as ours. But I was anxious about spending money. It's not that I feel like I have to ask for money, but I did feel like I had to justify what I spent. I've been home for a few years now, and spending money is no longer a problem for me. Ha ha. I had to come to terms, though, with the positive contributions I'm making for our family, regardless of monetary compensation. The kids are great; our family feels balanced.

Nancy, Mother of three
Skip, age 8
Jodi, age 7
Margo, age 2

*Read each "Point for reflection." Challenge yourself to answer the "tough" questions. Use these questions simply as a starting point; let your writing follow your thoughts. Take your time. And remember: Growth and change come slowly and are seldom easy.*

## POINTS FOR REFLECTION

List the emotional needs you meet for your family to which you cannot attach a dollar figure.

*1. Household manager*
*2. Xtra cur. activities for Kids.*
*3. Healthy eating habits*

> **Consider—** Perhaps you make a point to always be in the house when your kids get home from school in case they need to talk about something right away. Maybe you regularly go on a bike ride or make sure your children know you're there for them in other ways.

Talk with your partner about your specific concerns. Tell him that you feel like you need to justify what you spend or that you don't feel like it's yours to spend.

*N/A*

> **Consider—**Set a dollar limit above which you both agree to discuss a purchase before making it. Maybe it's $50 or $100.

How will you ensure that you maintain an equal financial partnership in your family?

*N/P*

> **Consider—**Pay the bills, make your household investments, start an investment club. Be involved.

## JEAN'S STORY

I will always work. Paid work is simply a part of me. My parents were divorced when I was 12 and I saw what my Mom went through. She had never been employed prior to the divorce, and it was devastating for her. She didn't know the first thing about finding a job. She didn't have a ton of skills. She hadn't ever even paid the bills. She didn't know the first thing about making investments. I vowed way back then that I would never depend on anyone else to support me financially. You just never know.

Jean, Mother of two

Carrie, age 9

Josh, age 5

## POINTS FOR REFLECTION

What are your core beliefs about work?

**Consider**—Is it the paycheck, is it a fulfilling part of your life? Is work a statement of power or status?

*I am still trying to decide that (6.27.02)*

What precautions could you take so that you wouldn't find yourself in a position like Jean's Mom?

**Consider**—Did you have a career before you were married? Do you currently pay the bills or make the investments for your family? At the very least, do you have a mental picture of your family finances?

Acknowledge that our Mothers lived in a different time and had less work experience and less money-related experience than we do. That said, list six job skills you could take to the street tomorrow if you wanted or needed to.

1. Good at working w/client, customers
2. Computer skills
3. Can work w/children.
4. Foreign language skills
5. Int. decorating & sawing.
6. Organizing
~ 7. Want to get into real estate

**Consider**—Children offer a wonderful battleground for negotiation, tolerance, patience, good listening skills. Have you gained experience in other areas through volunteer work? Could you?

Consider developing a marital agreement that essentially says that if your marriage dissolves, any assets you've accumulated during the marriage will be divided 50-50.

## TAYLOR'S STORY

I had always wanted to be a Mom! It's what I always dreamed of. Now that we have children, it doesn't look like we can make it on one income. Larry makes $50,000. I make roughly the same. Larry really wants me to stay home, too, so we're looking into how we could make this work. We've put off buying a big home just in case. Geez, though…$100,000 to $50,000…

Taylor, Mother of three

Mark, age 10
Caryn, age 4
Jodie, 8 months

## POINTS FOR REFLECTION

NOTE: There are many resources available if you're interested in investigating your estimated contribution to your family financial picture. Some are listed at the end of this chapter. Your personal accountant is a good resource as well.

Complete the form on page 57 to calculate how much of your salary you are actually contributing to your family's financial picture.

**Consider**—Many families are surprised to learn that childcare costs and the indirect costs of working often consume one income.

Are there ways for you to supplement your family income
while you're home with your children?

> **Consider**—Work out
> of your home or in a
> part-time position
> when your partner is
> home.

What material things are you and your partner willing to
sacrifice so that one of you might stay home with your
children?

> **Consider**—Are you
> accustomed to nice
> vacations? Eating out?
> Movies? Do you own
> your own home?

## GINA'S STORY

I've been home with our children since Kate was born nine years ago. With four kids, it's really busy. Greg and I haven't felt connected for what seems like forever. I'm scared for what would happen if we divorced. I have to believe he'd support the kids, but I'd certainly have to make huge changes, including finding paid work. I've been out of the job market for almost 10 years! What could I possibly do at this point? I think my name is on the mortgage and our cars—I don't even know that for sure. I pay the bills but don't know much about our investments or even if any are in my name. Would I be okay financially?

Gina, Mother of four

Carol-Jean, age 14
Amy, age 12
Tyler, age 10
Kate, age 9

## POINTS FOR REFLECTION

Look at past tax returns. Much personal and financial information can be gained, like annual wages, investment income, contributions to retirement plans.

**Consider**—If you don't know where your tax returns are, request them from your tax preparer or the IRS.

Obtain a copy of your husband's employee benefits. Employers will provide a written summary of benefits like life insurance protection, pension, profit sharing and 401(K) benefits, stock options, etc.

Contact an attorney to answer preliminary questions regarding your situation.

**Consider**—An attorney can explain alimony, child support, retirement benefits, and how your state laws affect these issues.

## ENDNOTES

1  Kelley, Linda. *Two Incomes and Still Broke?*, page vix.

2  © 1999 by Darcie Sanders and Martha Bullen. Reprinted with permission from *Staying Home: From Full-time Professional to Full-time Parent* (Spencer and Waters, revised 2001). For more information on Sanders' and Bullens' books, visit www.spencerandwaters.com, or e-mail: darcie@spencerandwaters.com.

3  McKenna, Elizabeth Perle. *When Work Doesn't Work Anymore: Women, Work, And Identity*, page 137.

## ADDITIONAL RESOURCES

### *Books*

*And What Do You Do?: When Women Choose to Stay Home*, by Loretta Kaufman and Mary Quigley

*It's Not the Glass Ceiling, It's the Sticky Floor and Other Things Our Daughters Should Know about Marriage, Work, and Motherhood*, by Karen Engberg, M.D.

*Staying Home: From Full-time Professional to Full-time Parent*, by Darcie Sanders and Martha Bullen.

*When Work Doesn't Work Anymore: Women, Work, And Identity*. McKenna, Elizabeth Perle.

### *Websites*

www.WIFE.org
   Women's Institute for Financial Education
   A non-profit organization dedicated to financial independence for women

www.financiallearning.com
   GE Center for Financial Learning
   Dedicated to educate and inform adults on the financial matters important in their lives

www.oxygen.com
   Ka-Ching
   Channel dedicated to money, business, and career

www.CNBC.com
CNBC.com Women's Investment Center
A comprehensive site written by women who are experts
in their respective finance-related fields

www.equalityinmarriage.org
Provides education to men and women about the importance of equality in marriage and divorce

www.spencerandwaters.com
Resources on parenting, at-home mothers, home-based
business, and other work/family issues to help balance
your life

## *Mailings*

*Love and Money: 150 Financial Tips for Couples*, by Kathleen Gurney,
Ph.D. and Ginita Wall, CPA, CFP. Send $5.00 and a self-
addressed stamped envelope with 55 cents postage to: WIFE,
10863 Vereda Sol Del Dios, San Diego, CA 92130.

# Chapter 5

## Long-term career implications: What happens next?

*"Often people attempt to live their lives backwards: They try to
have more things, or more money, in order to do more of what
they want so that they will be happier. The way it actually works is the
reverse. You must first be who you really are, then, do what you
need to do, in order to have what you want."*

Margaret Young

Maggie was asked to be full partner at her law firm. Susanna's considering stepping out of the workforce altogether. Marie's proposing a part-time option to her director. Delia's thinking of telecommuting, an option her employer has been offering for years. Shari's not sure what will happen to her future if she passes up another transfer.

The Mommy track, stepping out, job-sharing, sequencing—these phrases all imply a change in career status following the birth or adoption of a child or a career change that occurs as a result. The career implications of that change are dramatic, yet the quandary is simple: you've worked hard to establish yourself in a career. You are considering your work options. You may want to downsize your job or even step out for awhile, but are you committing professional suicide?

According to Mothers & More, a network for sequencing women, more than 70% of their membership plans to return to workplace in the future.[1] Madeleine Albright did it. Sandra Day O'Connor did it. Can you? Do you want to?

Researchers differ about how damaging time away or working less may be to a career. Workplace flexibility allows for reducing career involvement for some period of time, according to Catalyst, a non-profit research group.

The researchers contend that downshifting to part-time work won't necessarily derail your career.[2] A 1994 study of female MBAs, however, indicates otherwise, concluding that women taking even nine months away from full-time work were less likely to reach upper middle management positions than colleagues who worked continuously, and they made 17% less money even 10 years after they went back to work.

Although it's not clear how much taking time away or downsizing a job will affect your long-term career potential, one thing is certain: The career path you originally laid out is likely to significantly change if you step out. Arlene Cardozo's research noted that of the 350 women she interviewed who left full-time work to raise young children, only 10% said they would elect to return to a previous full-time corporate schedule. The other 90% found that they developed new self-perceptions and interests that extended far beyond their careers. When Cardozo asked them to rank-order terms regarding a second-time career decision, the ranking was no longer money, prestige, power, advancement, and security as it had been the first time around. Control over their own time and doing work that was fulfilling outweighed all other factors.[3]

Martha Farrell Erickson, Ph.D., Director of Children, Youth and Family Consortium at the University of Minnesota, stayed home with her children while they were young. She found that the time she spent as a Mother better equipped her as a professional and as a manager. "You have to be flexible and adaptable and sensitive if you're going to be a good parent. I've been thrilled with how that has played out in the workplace." I'd add patience, tolerance, and the art of negotiation to Dr. Erickson's list.

Should you choose to leave full-time employment for a period of time, there are ways to make yourself more marketable when it's time to go back. Here are a few ideas:
- Use this time to think about what you really *like* to do. Is there a way to make a career out of it?
- Identify skills that will transfer to another field.

- Target your volunteer activities to parallel your long-term interests.
- Take classes to stay current in your field. Also, read or do research on the Internet.
- Stay connected with colleagues—have lunch, dinner, or coffee occasionally.
- Build your network—you never know whom your new acquaintance from your son's kindergarten teacher knows.

Most of the women I interviewed who left full-time work now say that when they return to the paid workforce, they will be much more candid about what they're willing to give to their employer. They want to have a clear sense of balance in their lives, acknowledging that work is important but need not rule them. In general, they want to make sure a prospective employer offers—and encourages—employees to use family-friendly policies and offers alternative work arrangements. In fact, only 19% of the businesses surveyed by the Families & Work Institute's 1998 Business Work Life Study make a real and ongoing effort to inform employees of their work-life benefits.[4] It is also important to look at the leaders of the company. Do they take advantage of family-friendly policies?

I, for one, will no longer "sneak out" of work at 5:30 p.m. because corporate culture dictates I wait until my manager leaves first. I will be clear about how much time I'm willing to give to my job. If my daughter has a softball game at 5:00 or if I'm planning to meet my husband for an early dinner, I'll be there. If one of my children is sick, I'll tell my employer that my child is sick and stay home. It's that informal flexibility, the sense that I'm trusted to get my work done, that will attract me. Linda, part-time employee now after leaving an executive marketing position, insists she will never again bring work home. "How many nights I rushed to get Joey and Sandra to bed so that I could work on a project for work—it steams me to think about it. How many nights did I miss when they were babies? I need benefits, but I won't work more than 20 hours each week." Kate says that unless she can telecommute from home at least two days per week, she won't take the job.

Demanding? Unrealistic? I don't think so. We are searching for new definitions of work. We are creating tomorrow's work environment. We are creating the standards our children will live within. We, as women, are clearly not leaving the workforce. We comprise half of it. Companies today hire work-life managers who report to CEOs. They hire consultants to figure out how to retain qualified women. Millions of dollars fund huge studies by the Families & Work Institute, Wharton School of Business, and many other research groups. These expectations are fair for women, for all employees. Once we (men and women alike) speak the truth about the importance of family *and* work in our lives and follow through by living those values, corporate culture will be forced to continue to follow our lead in order to succeed in today's competitive marketplace. Women in college today fully expect to find a way to balance work and family obligations. They plan to maintain a paid work position and raise a family. They assume they will have collaborative partnerships. We are laying the groundwork for them to be able to succeed in their expectations.

## MAGGIE'S STORY

When my friends found out I was getting married, they were surprised. When they learned I was pregnant, they were stunned. When I told them I was jumping off the fast track for awhile, they nearly passed out.

As an attorney, it's not easy to practice in any way but all the way. After Jessica was born, though, everything about me changed. My priorities changed. It feels good, but it's also hard to modify the lifestyle I always thought I'd wanted. I pulled all the partners together and presented my proposal for part-time work with benefits, which, incidentally, no one before me had ever done. I was clear that someday I'd be back full-speed ahead, but that I needed my family now and my family needed me. They signed off on it. I may never get to the level I dreamed nor make the money my counterparts will, but above all, it feels right. I know I did the right thing.

Maggie, Mother of one
Jessica, age 1-1/2

*Read each "Point for reflection." Challenge yourself to answer the "tough" questions. Use these questions simply as a starting point; let your writing follow your thoughts. Take your time. And remember: Growth and change come slowly and are seldom easy.*

## POINTS FOR REFLECTION

List your professional goals. Will temporarily downsizing your job allow you to achieve these goals? What if you don't achieve your goals as you've laid them out?

List your personal goals. How do they relate to your professional goals?

**Consider**—Can your personal and professional goals exist together or are they mutually exclusive?

Re-design your job the way it would work best for you and your company.

**Consider**—What family-friendly policies are in place? Is there a precedent in your organization that you could learn from? Can you make it work?

Develop a proposal that describes your ideas for modifying your position.

**Consider**—Present it as a business proposal because that's what it is. Lay out the advantages for your employer rather than focusing on the benefits for you.

## MARTHA'S STORY

I think I want to stay home with my children. I just had my second child, Leland. I make about $40,000 a year but that's gone in a heartbeat after paying for childcare. I really like my job, though I do think staying home would be satisfying in a totally different way. But I'm scared that I wouldn't be as satisfied at home as I think I might. I also think I'd want to come back to my job in middle management—preferably at the same organization. Is this feasible at all? I feel like I'm making the biggest decision of my life.

Martha, Mother of two
Carly, age 9
Leland, age 5 months

## POINTS FOR REFLECTION

Would you consider a flexible work option such as telecommuting, job sharing, consulting, or a part-time option?

**Consider**—If you're working for reasons beyond money, such as self-fulfillment, recognition, or because you just like it, think about maintaining your career at some level.

What's the scariest part about quitting?

**Consider**—What would make it easier to consider those options? Explore alternative work arrangements.

How could you stay connected in your profession if you stayed home for a few years?

**Consider**—Could you take classes, have lunch frequently with co-workers, subscribe to industry journals?

## LAURIE'S STORY

I love my work. I've worked so hard to get where I am in my career that I feel like I can't get off-track now. I feel like I'd be wasting my education and experience and throwing away my career if I were to take few years off. I'd *never* re-enter at my level. I'd never be able to keep up with all that's changing in my industry. Sometimes I wish I had more time with my kids, but I don't really have a choice. My kids are fine. My husband and I work out the logistics each week. It works for us. Yet I do wonder what it would be like to live at a slower pace. I know that working 60 plus hours a week is a lot of time away from my family, but there's nothing I can do about it right now. I have to put it out of my mind.

Laurie, Mother of two
Kaitlin, age 7
Sean, age 4

## POINTS FOR REFLECTION

What are the top five priorities in your life? Rank them according to your emotional attachment or how strongly you feel about them. Now rank them according to how much time you spend tending to each. Is the time spent consistent with how much something/someone means to you?

**Consider**—Maybe your partner and your children mean the most to you, but you spend 80% of your time elsewhere.

According to your ranking above, do you need to look at your life right now and re-order the importance of your priorities?

**Consider**—Are there inconsistencies? If so, it's time to re-evaluate. What two steps will you take to begin living your priorities?
**Consider**—Take small steps first, like getting home from work a half-hour earlier two nights each week.

When you are with your children, are you fully present?

**Consider**—Do they have your full attention or are you multi-tasking other things at the same time? How will you give them your full attention? They know.

## JULIANA'S STORY

I've been home with Kiera for a year and just have to go back. I like being with her, but not all the time. I am so disillusioned about staying home full-time. I miss my old co-workers, I miss driving to work, I miss the intellectual challenge. I miss the daily adult interaction. I can't seem to connect with other women in a similar situation, so I'm home alone most of the time. Fred gets home at night and I feel like I have nothing interesting to say to him. I don't want to go back to working 65 hours a week, but a few would be nice. We could use the money, too.

Juliana, Mother of one
Kiera, age 2

## POINTS FOR REFLECTION

Did the company you were employed by offer any flexible work options? If so, would you be interested in returning?

Brainstorm three different work options that would satisfy your desire to work part-time.

**Consider**—How would you feel about telecommuting, starting a small business, or working part-time?

Do you feel like you're looking for a job as a distraction from home or as an intellectual exercise?

**Consider**—It will be much easier to find a job that offers a distraction from your child(ren) than it is to find an intellectually challenging position within your parameters. To find a job that truly challenges you yet fits within your parameters will be more difficult. It's not impossible, but more difficult.

## ENDNOTES

1   Mothers & More website, www.mothersandmore.org

2   Catalyst. 1995. *A New Approach to Flexibility*, pages 52-53.

3   Cardozo, Arlene Rossen. *Sequencing: Having It All but Not All at Once: A New Solution for Women Who Want Marriage, Career, and Family*, page 217.

4   Families and Work Institute. *1998 Business Work-Life Study: Managing the Work/Time Equation*, page viii.

## ADDITIONAL RESOURCES

### *Websites*

www.catalystwomen.org
   Catalyst
   A non-profit organization working with business and the professions to effect change for women

www.workoptions.com
   Working Mothers' resource for negotiating flexible work

www.mothersandmore.org
   A website designed for sequencing Mothers

http://www.awlp.org
   Alliance of Work/life professionals. Membership organization that promotes work/family and personal life balance.

www.fastcompany.com
   e-version of the magazine of the same name, working to chronicle how changing companies create and compete, to highlight new business practices, and to showcase the teams and individuals who are inventing the future and reinventing business

# Chapter 6

## Striving for work and family balance: Why can't we just be?

*"Learn to get in touch with the silence within yourself and know that everything in this life has a purpose."*

Elizabeth Kubler-Ross

I might as well just say it. You can't fit everything in and enjoy it. OK—I said it. Oh, and there's really no such thing as balance. Balance implies that you may actually get there—like maybe next Tuesday at 10:00. Balance will always elude you. You *can*, however, make intentional decisions about how you will spend your time so that you can feel that your life and work have value. You can be intentional about how many hours each day you work, and how much time you spend being fully present with each child. You can be intentional about the commitments you make outside your family. The choices are yours.

As working parents, we know we don't have as much time as we'd like with our children. According to a study conducted by *Fast Company* magazine, 87% of those surveyed really want more balance between their work life and their personal life and believe they can achieve it if they're willing to make some trade-offs. Yet when they were honest with themselves, the reasons for not working to create that balance ranged from, "I don't want to have to make trade-offs," to "It feels good to be as busy as I am now," to "I'm not willing to give up money or material things," to "I like to be known for working long and hard."[1]

You're not off the hook if you're home with your children. Balance is still a challenge. Concentrated time with a child is often postponed with a "just a minute" because housework, volunteer work, meal-making, soccer, piano, and feeding the baby take front stage. The at-home Mother who starts out looking for companionship and "something to do" will network, volunteer, and help her children get involved in activities. Pretty soon, she'll go from talking to the long-distance telemarketer at 4:30 p.m. just so she can hear another adult voice to being busier than she'd like. And if she has a partner who typically works longer and harder to accelerate his career and to compensate for the loss of an income because he doesn't have to worry about child-care issues, time still falls far short of "enough."

We live in an insanely busy world fueled by laptops, Palm Pilots®, cell phones, the Internet, beepers, television, VCRs, DVDs, and more. Whether or not you're employed has little to do with busy days and overscheduling. Society rewards busy-ness—both monetarily and emotionally. Our media encourage it. The adrenaline rush maintains it. It's easy in this, the 21st century, to be in touch no matter what, at any time of the day or night, with everyone but ourselves. That is the reality that technology creates in our lives.

One impact of all this technology is referred to as "integration" by Wall Street Journal columnist Sue Schellenbarger.[2] In this context, integration refers to the graying of lines between work and home so that you can have more time with your family, with the understanding that work can reach you and you can reach work anytime. Integration holds many advantages for the workplace. There are personal advantages too, like flexibility, but actually getting away from work—literally and figuratively—becomes far more difficult than before.

When your world is busy, regardless of work status, it's easier to follow the path of least resistance and just keep plugging along. Dawn left a high-level marketing position to be home more with her son, Luke. She said, "Looking back on it all (and knowing how I feel now when I'm truly enjoying the moment with Luke), I'm not sure I ever fully decompressed after a busy day at work. My job flew 100 mph all day long, and although I had a 45-minute drive home, my head was still moving at about 70 mph thinking about project solutions, etc. I tried, but it was difficult."

Linda compared her experience to feeling like she was on a treadmill and there was no (slow) down button. "I did the things that meant a lot, but that meant I literally ran at 3:30 a.m. I finally took a leave of absence, then quit. The first Saturday after I'd resigned, (my son) Taylor came and said, 'Don't we have to go on errands?' You realize you weren't the only one at this pace. You don't realize how fast you're going until you stop."

Bette notes that she "could shift gears but never really relax. I bet I never relaxed for about five years. And what I found was an inability to focus on the moment. When I was driving the kids, I was writing a chapter of my dissertation in my head. When I was 'working' outside the home, I spent all that time thinking about the kids. It was crazy."

A friend of mine hired a personal coach, Marty Mumma, who asked her frequently, "Why must you always do; why can't you just be?" To have a sense of balance, a feeling of inner harmony, there must be downtime; there must be time just to be. I interviewed many women, employed and at home, who were so busy with their schedules and the schedules of their children that they never took time just to be. Eddie Cantor said once, "Slow down and enjoy life. It's not only the scenery you miss by going too fast—you miss the sense of where you are going and why."

Each of us must be deliberate about living the values most important us, not the values that slide by in our society. If you aren't clear about your values and how you must honor them, how will you and your family know when you are living up to them? It's important to evaluate the busy-ness occasionally and make sure you are living your life and modeling the values you want to pass on. But it's not just the busy-ness; it's the busy-ness without direction or goals. You know what both feel like. There's the fast pace that makes you feel like you're in a groove and feels good. Then there's the fast pace that makes you feel like you're just chasing your tail.

Setting clear boundaries is paramount to intentionality. You must be consciously aware of your need for space and your energy. Realize that you have the right—no, the responsibility—to protect your privacy, to not over-schedule your children, to find quiet time for yourself. It's ok not to answer your phone or respond to e-mail messages right away. You can change your mind. Respect yourself.

As a woman in our chaotic society, you need to practice saying "No" in order to quiet the pace of your life enough to have quiet time with your partner, your children, yourself. Try it:

NO, I CANNOT SERVE ON ANOTHER CHURCH COMMITTEE.

NO, I DON'T HAVE TIME TO VOLUNTEER IN JOE'S CLASS THIS MONTH!

NO, I DON'T HAVE TO VACUUM TODAY.

Try it little-by-little—the easy ones first. You will find that your friends are still your friends, your children's school will still be their school, your church will still be your church. They will understand—perhaps be a bit envious that you found a way to say no when they didn't! And you might have time to play Monopoly with your son, catch balls with your daughter, write in your journal, read the paper with your partner with quiet music playing in the background, or just sit quietly, giving thanks for all that you have.

Although we are usually not consciously aware of our choices, we all make numerous decisions each day regarding how we spend our time and with whom. Intentionality is the key to feeling some semblance of balance. At any given time, your many roles are in flux. Be deliberate in where you spend your time and how you go about fulfilling the passions in your life.

## MARY ELLEN'S STORY

I feel like this just keeps getting harder and more intense. My career is really demanding, but I love it. My husband, Mark, is great. I adore my kids. When I got my first cell phone, I was excited beyond belief at what I thought would make my life so much easier. I'll call back clients during my commute and get so much more done, I reasoned. I still like that the kids can reach me, but I never really get away from work. I negotiated two days of working at home, which certainly has its benefits, but there's nothing stopping me from checking e-mails every night and on weekends or my co-workers from calling any time. I'm up late working on projects after the kids are in bed. I accepted an appointment on a community board. I volunteer in my children's classrooms. It never, ever stops and I don't know what to do about it anymore. I'm fried. I can't remember the last time I worked out. If I do have a couple of hours alone, I need only look around the house for a nanosecond before finding something needing to be done. My life is full of things I have to do. I never seem to get to the things I want to do.

Mary Ellen, Mother of three
Charlie, age 12
Mary, age 9
Chad, age 7

*Read each "Point for reflection." Challenge yourself to answer the "tough" questions. Use these questions simply as a starting point; let your writing follow your thoughts. Take your time. And remember: Growth and change come slowly and are seldom easy.*

## POINTS FOR REFLECTION

List the five highest priorities in your life.

**Consider**—Is it your children, your partner, God or another Higher Power, exercise, a big house, boat, health, dog, managing 500 people?

Are you spending appropriate amounts of time on the priorities you listed above?

**Consider**—If not, why not? Look at your calendar. Do you need to re-evaluate your priorities? What are your family's perceptions? **Ask them**.

What are the five things you most want your kids to remember about their childhood?

**Consider**—What values are most important? Are you supporting those values (i.e., integrity, honesty, spirituality, sense of humor) in the way that *you* live each day?

What's your hidden payoff for leading such a chaotic life?

**Consider**—Do you want others to perceive you as a workaholic, too busy to rest, satisfied with five hours of sleep each night?

## TRUDI'S STORY

I find I don't take much time for friends anymore. I have a core group of friends I stayed in touch with for years. Now, I don't take the time because I'm emotionally and physically drained. After working all day, then "turning it on" for Seth in the evening, I'm just plain done by 9:00 p.m. Some nights I don't even want to talk to my husband, Jeff. When an old friend calls in the evening, I often pretend not to be home. On weekends, I just want to be with my family and cut myself off from everything else. I find myself waiting to turn everything off and just be. The only time I can "just be," though, is when I'm in bed....sleeping. So, I miss my friends. I miss feeling like I'm there for them. I really feel like a bad friend; sometimes I feel like a bad daughter, too. I miss too many birthdays. The saddest thing of all, I think, is that we're all so busy that they forget, too.

Trudi, Mother of one
Seth, age 4

## POINTS FOR REFLECTION

How could you be creative in the ways you stay in touch with friends and family?

**Consider**—Keep note-cards, your address book, and pictures of your children in your purse or briefcase. When you have a spare moment, waiting for an appointment or your child to finish an activity, write a quick note. Send one personal e-mail each day before you begin your workday.

All Mothers sacrifice something to strike the balance they think is right for them. What sacrifices have you made to strike your work/life balance?

**Consider**—Is your sacrifice working? Are you doing all the giving?

Pull out your calendar. Yes—Go grab it now. Make seven columns on a sheet of paper. At the top of each column, write one of your roles (such as Mother, partner, employee, friend, spiritual individual, volunteer, daughter). From the information in your calendar, record how much time you've spent in each of these roles in the past two weeks.

**Consider**—Are you spending time on things that are truly important to you?

What am I missing by being so busy?

**Consider**—What would a sense of quiet give me? Am I afraid to be quiet?

## CAROLINE'S STORY

I feel like I'm just going through the motions these days. I move like a robot from one activity or commitment to the next—bring the kids here, fly there, get dinner ready because soccer's early tonight, finish writing my presentation. I don't know what made me start thinking about it—I wish I hadn't—but please tell me there's more to life than this. Others look at me and say I have a good life, and I suppose I do. I just don't have time to enjoy it. I have a great husband and good kids, my job is fine, but it doesn't seem like anything really means that much. It's scary to think my life might be half over and I'm still trying to figure out what I'm supposed to be doing. We just run from one thing to the next.

> Caroline, Mother of three
>
> Angie, age 11
> Tony, age 8
> Sara, age 5

## POINTS FOR REFLECTION

Be sure to frame your situation realistically. Caroline comments that she doesn't have the time to enjoy her life as it is now. In reality, Caroline doesn't *take* the time. She is not being deliberate about her choices. Are you? How would you frame your personal situation today in terms of busy-ness?

If you identify with Caroline, you are on some sort of journey. It's time to step back and really look at your life.

> **Consider**—Can you go away alone for a few days or a couple of weeks and think about yourself with regard to your personal relationships, your work, your spirituality, your own needs?

Keep a journal every day. A journal can be tremendously revealing after just a couple of months of writing.

**Consider**—Writing will truly help you clarify your path.

What memories do you want your children to have about these years (the day-to-day memories, not those that come from travel and big events)? Are you doing everything in your power to create those memories?

**Consider**—Perhaps you want your children to remember that Saturday morning is "pancake morning" because you and your husband always make pancakes for breakfast. Perhaps you want them to remember that you always took a walk in the neighborhood together after dinner.

## CARMEN'S STORY

I've been home with my children for four years now. The first year or so was AWFUL! I loved my job and it was hard to leave, but I felt strongly about being with my kids for a few years—for them and for me. During that first year, I cried a lot. All of my friends still worked and I was incredibly lonely. I didn't know anyone else who was home with his or her children. I felt unproductive and insignificant. I was alone way too much. My husband, Jon, tried to understand but couldn't really—I didn't even understand. So, now? Now I feel like I'm going 90 mph all day and all evening. Between the kids' activities, what seems like countless volunteer hours at school and at church, and keeping up the house, I'm fried. I was so desperate at first to do something that I said "yes" to everyone who asked me for something. Now, I feel trapped in all of the expectations there seem to be. Jon keeps telling me just to say no now, but it's hard. I don't want to hurt anyone's feelings or have a project dropped because I'm unwilling to help. I'm not having fun, though. And, bottom line, I don't have nearly enough time to just be with the kids or with Jon. If I have this little time with them, I might as well go back to earning a paycheck for it.

Carmen, Mother of three

Tara, age 12
Brad, age 10
Kirin, age 5

## POINTS FOR REFLECTION

Make a list of your monthly commitments using your scheduling calendar.

**Consider**—Some examples might include: Johnny's school 4 hours a month; Tim's school 4 hours a month; "Women's Neighborhood Night Out" 3 hours a month; church committee 1 hour meeting plus 4 hours work a month; Board of Directors for bank 3 hours a month.

From your list above, what one or two activities could you say no to right now?

**Consider**—Pick up the phone and call the appropriate person now and say no.

Establish a weekly family night.

> **Consider**—Let the children take turns planning it. Depending on family activities, it may need to be scheduled a different night each week. That's OK, but keep the commitment sacred.

When someone calls to ask you to volunteer or help him or her out, how do you respond?

> **Consider**—Make it a personal policy never to say "yes" or "no" on the spot. That gives you time to really think about the commitment and whether it fits in with your family.

## ENDNOTES

[1] "How Much is Enough," *Fast Company Magazine*, July-August, 1999, Issue 261, page 110.

[2] Sue Shellenbarger, *Wall Street Journal*, February 18, 1998.

## ADDITIONAL RESOURCES

### Books

*Slowing Down to the Speed of Life*, by Richard Carlson and Joseph Bailey

### Websites

www.thirdpath.org
The ThirdPath Institute
A non-profit organization dedicated to helping people
redesign work to create time for other life priorities

# Chapter 7

## Becoming whole, staying whole: Taking care of yourself.

*"Is this then what happens to woman? She wants perpetually to spill herself away. All her instinct as a woman—the eternal nourisher of children, of men, of society—demands that she give. Her time, her energy, her creativeness drain out into these channels if there is any chance, any leak. Traditionally we are taught, and instinctively we long, to give where it is needed—and immediately. Eternally, woman spills herself away in driblets to the thirsty, seldom being allowed the time, the quiet, the peace, to let the pitcher fill up to the brim."*

Anne Morrow Lindbergh, *from* Gift From the Sea

*Or,*
*"If Mama ain't happy, ain't nobody happy."*

Rick Hennighausen

**"** f Mama ain't happy, ain't nobody happy." It's true. I fought the label for years. In fact, when Rick first said it, I'd cringe. But 11 years of marriage and three children later, I accept the fact that he's right. It's humbling or flattering or something to realize that as the Mother, you likely set the tone for your family. You have the ability to make rainy days special. You kiss the "ow-ies." You're the one who drops everything when your adolescent is ready to confide in you. You comfort and counsel in a way only a Mother can. You're the center. If you're home full-time, you're the center. If you work part-time, you're the center. If you work full-time, you're the center. I even talked to a woman whose partner stays home with their children and she's *still* the center. Like it or not, the pressure's on. And unless you feel fulfilled and satisfied in *your* life, you won't be at your very best for your family.

"To be better parents, Moms need to make the choice to take time for themselves and they need the support of their spouses and their employers and society as a whole to do so," says Stewart Friedman in his book, *Work and Family—Allies or Enemies.*[1] It's hard to carve out time for yourself.

99

Household tasks, paid work, volunteer work, children, partner, parents, friends, church—there's so much to do. Finding time to nourish your own soul and refill the proverbial well must be a high priority or it will get lost in the list of other things you must do. Consider it a personal responsibility.

The notion of taking care of yourself involves both physical and emotional components. Physically, you take care of yourself through exercise, proper amounts of sleep, and good nutrition, all of which are essential but are not the subject of this book. In the context of this book, taking care of yourself refers to feeding the spirit and finding ways to make you genuinely happy.

There are two levels at which each of us must take care of ourselves. You will intuitively recognize both as they are described even though you may not have ever looked at them this way.

1. The first level addresses the short-term need to get away from the situation you are in. It may be a bad day at the office; it may be a horrible afternoon at home. You know the feeling. The kids are loud; they're not listening. They're not picking up on your frustration. Or, your project proposal at work gets turned down, the politics are out of control, and you're all tied up in knots. Getting away is the best answer for everyone.

   Finding time to go for a run or call a friend or read a book or get a massage will usually satisfy this short-term need for a break. Finding ways to carve out an hour here or there is usually fairly easy with a little creative planning. If you and a friend like to run, for instance, swap kids for an hour three times each week or run together using running strollers (and lots of snacks) for the kids. Reading is good because you can do it at home or over your lunch hour whenever a quiet moment presents itself. Maybe your break is channel surfing or surfing the web. The goal in these moments of coping is to simply to distract yourself from what you are currently finding stressful. The challenge, then, is to not allow yourself to be distracted by dirty dishes, ten waiting e-mails, or the not-at-all-planned dinner.

2. The second level of taking care of yourself involves finding something that fulfills you at a much deeper level. This is a great challenge, of course—you'll need to create the space to work, physically and mentally, as well as find the support you'll need to make it work.

Kathleen's son is a diabetic. She wants to do everything she can for him and to help find a cure for this disease. She's immersed herself in fundraising where her career as an advertising executive has helped make her quite a success. Kathleen feels tremendously fulfilled personally. She's filling her need to have something she can call her own while contributing a great deal to her community!

Sarah works as an interior designer. She loves everything about it—choosing fabrics, furniture, meeting with clients—everything. The bonus is that she gets paid for it! So, for Sarah, her passion is her work. Perfect.

What is it that makes you feel passionate? There is a talent, a gift, a passion, perhaps waiting idly, to be discovered, and when you discover your passion, you may feel overwhelmed. So many obstacles face us. Women who've worked at it will tell you that, yes, it's really hard to set up the support you'll need, and it's a lot of work to be so organized with your time and focused on a project, but it is SO worth it The feeling that you're doing something for yourself is amazing. To know in your heart that you're doing something you absolutely love will carry you a long way.

One of the challenges is, of course, developing a support system. You might talk to your partner about giving each other time each week to pursue your respective passions. Perhaps you take the kids one night a week from 4:30 until 9:00 p.m. and he takes them another evening. If you can make it your passion and get paid for it, consider hiring part-time childcare. Consider getting a babysitter one night a week so that each of you can do his/her own thing. Think about putting the kids to bed early a night or two a week with a movie or coloring supplies and work for two or three hours (which is, by the way, how this book was written).

One of my best friends, Kathy, has seven children under the age of 11. Yes. Seven children under the age of 11. Kathy has many talents, one of which is photography. She and another friend, Dawn, started a children's photography business. Kathy says she can do that because it doesn't take a lot of time away from home and she has support from her husband, Jim, as well as her friends. Is it challenging sometimes? Of course it is. Is it worth it? Unquestionably. Here's the benefit from Kathy's point of view: "Photography gives me so much. I spend time with my business partner, who is a good friend, doing something I'm passionate about—creating and preserving family memories! I think it's important to have time away from my kids to re-energize, and it's good for them to have me away sometimes. I also think they (the kids) need to know that I have outside interests. Last—and truly least for me—I may even make a little money at it."

As you begin to discover your passion, consider the following:

**Determine what you want to do.**

Maybe it's writing or training for a marathon or learning French or taking a computer class. Maybe it's looking at a profession you've always been interested in. It doesn't matter what you choose, but it must excite you. And, most importantly, it has to be yours—not your partner's or your children's. Yours.

**Schedule sacred time.**

Marty Mumma, a personal coach, calls them "Magic Marker Moments." Put them in your schedule. Marty suggests drawing a big, colorful X with a highlighter through the block of time you're saving for yourself to help encourage yourself to keep that time sacred.

**Make a plan.**

How many times have you finally made time to do something for yourself and when the hour you set aside begins, you think, "OK, what should I do? I only have 60 minutes. Maybe I should run to the store. No, no I have to do something for me. Maybe read a book. What book should I read? I'll just fold this one load of laundry and then I'll decide…" Prior to your sacred time, write down your plan in your datebook or at least make mental notes so you know exactly what will happen the first minute.

**Avoid distractions.**

Although it is time for you, hold it dear as though it was paid work (and good for you if it is!) That way, you may be less inclined to do that quick load of laundry, take just a couple of minutes to vacuum, or make a quick trip to the store.

I asked a number of women how they find time to take care of themselves. Here's what some of them said:

☎ "My husband and I joined an athletic club with great child care facilities. Our son loves going to the child care center, as there are so many fun things to play with, and I can get in a good work-out—which totally revives me."
—Dawn, Mother of Luke (age 5)

☎ "I can't always rely on outside support since Mark frequently travels and I'm not comfortable asking friends to watch Robby (our son) while I work out or work on one of my craft projects. So, I have found that when Robby sleeps I can find extended periods of time when I can do things for me."
—Cheryl, Mother of Robby (age 2)

☎ "My Mother has an uncanny sense about those precise moments when I've reached the end of my rope, and she always seems to know when I need bailing out."
—Amy, Mother of D.J. (age 8) and Valerie (age 4)

☎ "I read on the express bus to work, I skip a little sleep to walk my dog alone in the early morning, or write in my journal."
—Amy, Mother of Sam (age 11) and Nate (age 5)

☎ "Does going to sleep at night count?"
—Sara, Mother of Heidi (age 7) and Marie (age 9)

## MARIAN'S STORY

Between working from home part-time, getting the kids to their activities, helping them with homework and Gene's travel schedule, it usually feels impossible to carve out time for myself. By the end of the night, I just want to sit, watch TV, and not think anymore. When I'm not exhausted, I feel like I should do some work. I have a good life, but I feel like there's a piece missing. When Gene's home, I'm not anxious to leave because we really like spending time together. Yet I often feel like there's nothing in it for me right now. I know I need to take better care of myself, but I don't know how anymore.

Marian, Mother of two

Marty, age 8
Steven, age 4

*Read each "Point for reflection." Challenge yourself to answer the "tough" questions. Use these questions simply as a starting point; let your writing follow your thoughts. Take your time. And remember: Growth and change come slowly and are seldom easy.*

## POINTS FOR REFLECTION

If you identify with Marian, you need to work at both levels of taking care of yourself. At a simple level, list three activities that divert your attention from everyday concerns or stresses.

**Consider**—Television is a diversion, but not a particularly healthy one. What about taking a walk, reading a book, writing a letter?

On a deeper level, you must look at ways to fill your soul. Perhaps your work does that. If not, brainstorm five hobbies/talents/interests that have gotten away from you in this phase of your life. Which could you do at home in 1-3 hour chunks?

**Consider**—If you carve out a few hours each week and schedule them into your day, you will discover or rediscover a talent which will fulfill you.

How will you carve out the time? Where will you find the support?

**Consider**—Put the kids to bed early with paper and markers or books once or twice each week. Barter with a neighbor or friend for alone time—you care for her kids in exchange for her caring for yours. Or, hire a babysitter for a few hours while your partner is out of town.

## LINDA'S STORY

It's pretty easy for me to set time aside. Our kids are in
school. I do a lot of volunteer work, but it's mostly on my
schedule. It's easy for me to go for a walk or have coffee with
a friend. But what I really want is to train for a marathon. I
run a little bit now—maybe two or three miles. When I think
about doing it, I get excited but terribly overwhelmed. I look
around the house and I see everything else I should do. How
can I justify training so intensely when there's laundry and
grocery shopping to do, dinner to prepare, and all the rest? It
feels too big for me. So I never start. But I feel it inside. I
don't know where to begin.

Linda, Mother of three

Joanie, age 12
Kery, age 10
Jordyn, age 8

## POINTS FOR REFLECTION

If you had three solid hours to yourself, how would you fill
them? What dreams, interests, or hobbies do you think
you'd enjoy?

**Consider**—Remember
when you were a child.
What did you like to
do? Don't think about
obstacles.

What steps do you need to take in order to get yourself set up in your hobby or interest?

> **Consider**—List all of the steps and set up realistic timelines for yourself. When you break a project into manageable tasks, it's not nearly as over-whelming. Take small, yet fulfilling, steps.

Where will you look for support in household chores or what will you say no to in order to free up some time for yourself?

> **Consider**—Order dinner in once a week, give your children additional chores, hire a housecleaner, ask your partner to cook once a week.

## MARLENE'S STORY

I never seem to get to the part where I take care of myself. I meet—even anticipate—the needs of my family. I fulfill my outside obligations. I work out at 5:30 a.m. four times per week. I'm a mortgage lender and work about 40 hours a week. I do the dishes, the laundry, the floors. I feed the dog, get the kids to soccer, give my partner an occasional backrub. By the time 9:30 or 10:00 rolls around and I could start thinking about me, I am done. Beat. I miss time for me a lot. It took me awhile to realize that it was missing from my life, but now I know. I need it. My patience runs low. One day, I talked to my husband, Craig. I told him that I needed time for me, too. He looked at me like I was a bit strange and could see that this somehow involved him, but asked me how he could help. I carved out time for me and he supports me in that. It feels a lot better. It doesn't always work and I don't always get away, but it's so much better than it was. I feel like a better Mother, for sure. And a better partner, friend.

Marlene, Mother of three
Scott, age 9
Shelly, age 6
Sam, age 3

## POINTS FOR REFLECTION

Remember when you had significant time for yourself (probably before kids)? What did you do with that time?

**Consider**—Brainstorm a list of activities and pastimes you remember enjoying.

Do you have a friend or acquaintance who seems to really take good care of herself?

> **Consider**—Talk to her about how she does it. See if any of her strategies would work for you.

Make a plan...write down the steps. How (specifically) will you find the time to incorporate something for you into your life?

> **Consider**—Talk to your partner, co-op baby-sit with a friend, enlist a family member's help.

## DRADAE'S STORY

I began staying home with my children when my third, Julia, was born. I had a great career and I loved it, but it just got to be too much for our whole family. My husband, Dan, and I discussed who would stay home. He was willing too, but I felt like I was more ready. It was super hard at first. I found myself getting really angry with the kids for pretty goofy things. I knew I was sorting through a lot emotionally, so I saw a psychologist for awhile. She asked me during one session what my kids do that angers me so. It was just regular kids' stuff—not getting ready for school fast enough, not doing their chores, not picking up. What I realized is that I was angry because I had no time for myself and felt like I just kept doing the same things over and over and over. Then came the clincher. She asked me what I'd be doing instead. I thought a long sentence with tons of ideas was ready to spill out but—nothing. I hadn't looked for anything to make me happy yet. I hadn't re-discovered any hobbies or outside interests. Finding things I was truly interested in made all the difference for me and for my family.

Dradae, Mother of three

Maggie, age 9
Jodi, age 4
Julia, age 1

## POINTS FOR REFLECTION

Is there a cause you are passionate for? Brainstorm how you will express that passion in a way that emphasizes a greater good.

**Consider**—Is it literacy, school board, fund-raising for the new library, homelessness in your community?

What is your first step in getting started in your effort to fulfill that passion?

> **Consider**—Do you know anyone involved in the area you are interested in? Does your church have a connection? Your child's school? The library?

Do you have a friend, colleague, or family member who has a new interest you admire?

> **Consider**—Take him/her for coffee and talk about the interest or hobby. Read about it. Is it something you want to experiment with?

## ENDNOTES

[1] Friedman, Stewart D. and Jeffrey H. Greenhaus. *Work and Family—Allies or Enemies*. page 80.

## ADDITIONAL RESOURCES

### Books

*The Artist's Way*, by Julia Cameron
*Good Enough Mothers: Changing Expectations for Ourselves*, by Melinda M. Marshall
*Surrendering to Motherhood: Losing Your Mind, Finding Your Soul*, by Iris Krasnow

### Websites

www.Networkingmoms.com
Networking Moms
Natalie Graham, personal coach, shares her philosophies and practical approach to living life with truth and honesty

www.oxygen.com
Oxygen powers a television station and a website for and about women. There are channels covering issues from finances (ka-ching) to personal relationships.

# Afterword

## It's over in a blink:
## Pearls of wisdom from our mothers.

*"How did it get so late so soon?*
*It's night before it's afternoon.*
*December is here before it's June.*
*My goodness, how the time has flewn.*
*How did it get so late so soon?"*

Dr. Seuss

I had a remarkable grandmother. Her name was Ethyl Hoida and she was born in 1909. In 1935, she opened a dress shop called *Ethyl's Dress Shop: A Bit of 5th Avenue* to help support her family during obviously difficult economic times. My Mom feels like she grew up in that dress shop, from the time she fit in a bassinet to the times much later when she traveled with my Grandma by train from Green Bay, Wisconsin to Chicago on buying trips.

Grandma Hoida died of cancer in my Mom's home a few years ago. Now a guest room, "Grandma's room" is seldom used for guests and contains countless remembrances. Old photographs hang on the walls and sit on her bed stand, costume jewelry adorns her dresser, various knick-knacks describe her incredible and eccentric personality. A pile of hymnals and prayer books remind me of her strong faith. As I recently browsed through them, I came across a book, *Why Women Cry or Wenches With Wrenches*, by Elizabeth Hawes, published in 1943. It begins, "This book is addressed to all women who have ever felt that if, without a vacation of some sort, they must wash that dish, iron that shirt, cook that meal, see that child, kiss that husband again, they would go mad." Why is it that my jaw dropped at the thought that women in 1943 felt the same way I do some days? How I flatter myself thinking we are so different. In my somewhat naïve and romantic view, I suppose I thought that my Grandma, her friends, and her neighbors were somehow more accepting of the expectations others held. I found a peaceful sense of irony in realizing that, when that book was published, women struggled with many of the very issues covered in the book you now hold.

I wish my Grandma were alive so I could tell her about my book and thank her for the part she played in paving the way for me to have the opportunity to make the difficult choices I can make today. I wish I could hear her laugh, her hand daintily covering the teeth she didn't like while her eyes filled with glistening tears, at the thought that we think our struggles today are so different than those she dealt with more than 60 years ago.

My Grandma and so many others faced the challenges of equality for women; they stood tall, insisting that we can play as significant a role in society as men, forcing change—little by little. Cultural variables change over time as the role of men, women, children, work, and many other social institutions change. However, the core issues have not changed from the years when my Grandma had her dress shop and today. Hawes discusses balance, how important it is for women to take care of themselves, and cultural expectations in ways that reflect a different culture yet mirror the struggles you and I encounter today.

## PEARLS OF WISDOM

This final chapter considers the wisdom and perspective of ten women I interviewed in the spring of 2000. These women share the wisdom and perspective that come from experiencing the endless conflicts between work and family and balance 15 or 20 years ago. Some of the women I talked with worked part-time or full-time for pay, some were home full-time with their children. Only one thought was shared by all:

> The years your children are home are over in a blink.
> They're gone in a heartbeat. Don't have regrets.

When I spent time with these ten women, they didn't want to talk about who made "the best" work/life choices or which choice was best. Some of the women I spoke with didn't feel they could leave the workforce at all because they could never have re-entered at a comparable level in their competitive field. Others stayed in the work force part-time; still others left the workforce altogether for some time. All are devoted to their families and happily spoke of the close relationships they have with their children today. Each had the best interest of their families in mind all along the way. Gail MarksJarvis, business columnist and award-winning journalist at the *St. Paul Pioneer Press*, left the work force for six months after the birth of her first child and quipped, "I had to find an easier job." Profoundly, though, Gail said this: "Think about how you'll meet your child's needs first. It doesn't mean you have to be there to meet all of her needs; it just means you make sure they are met."

Through my conversations with these wise women, three themes revealed themselves:
- Be deliberate about your path.
- Sometimes you have to buck the system.
- Take care of yourself.

## BE DELIBERATE ABOUT YOUR PATH.

"Take time periodically to evaluate your course," Mary Mahoney stated very clearly. "Life is about choices. Don't think it's not. You make decisions every day about how you'll spend your time: with whom, for how long, at what expense." Mary struck me as a very deliberate person herself. She has clearly listened to her voice throughout her successful career as an entrepreneur. She listened to her own voice as it told her to leave 20 years in corporate America. She felt the tug to start her own business and did. She listened— really listened—when her children boycotted after-school care because they thought they were old enough to be home alone (which is when Mary began creating flexible jobs for herself), and she listened to her creative voice in launching a very different organization. Mary is founder and president of LeadersCircle LLC, a leadership development and consulting services firm, which specializes in developing the "people" side of organizations.

Being deliberate means taking time to listen. Mary describes what she's termed "the Gerbil Wheel of Life." She maintains that if you stay on the Gerbil Wheel of Life, moving at the fast pace of life around and around and around to work and children's sports and piano and dinner engagements and manicures, that you don't take time to look at the most important things in your life. And sometimes when you stop and look, you see things about yourself you'd rather not see. But seeing those scary things is part of the process. In order to know yourself, accept yourself, and love yourself, you must look at yourself—even the parts you don't really like. It's difficult to take the blinders off and really look at your priorities only to find that you're not honoring those you name as most important.

Mary Dee Hicks, Ph.D., former Senior Vice President at Performance Decisions International, agrees with Mary Mahoney. Mary Dee quit her job cold turkey after reaching a level in her job she always thought she was working toward. Having achieved it, though, she described an experience of not recognizing who she was. "She's not who I thought she'd be and not who I wanted her to be." So, after a short period of consideration, she quit. Mary Dee tells us, "Do not be afraid of what seems like drastic change. As radical a change as I thought I was making...well, I woke up and my children were still my children, my husband my husband, my house was still my house. And my personality traits and characteristics always remained intact."

Martha Erickson, Ph.D., Director of the University of Minnesota's Children, Youth and Family Consortium, says she's, "kind of amazed at how things 'turned out.'" While others in her world of academia encouraged her to follow the expected teaching and research route and even suggested she might be compromising her career, she kept her priorities in order, carving out positions that were "less than full-time." It worked out well for Dr. Erickson, who now speaks internationally and consults with former Vice President Al Gore regarding family issues.

## SOMETIMES YOU HAVE TO BUCK THE SYSTEM.

A few of the women I spoke with talked in depth about fighting the notion of what others think you ought to be doing. Barb Smith, an elementary school teacher and mother of two grown daughters, said, "you have to buck the system. Society conditions us—you're significant if you're making lots of money and formally using your education. You have much less value if you leave the workforce. Be careful. Evaluate your choices and don't hurry them."

Linda Kelly, stay-at-home mother of three grown children, agrees with Barb. If you choose to be home with your children full-time, "Don't be a martyr. Because there are no monetary rewards for staying at home with our children, many of us look for praise and assurance from spouses that what we are doing is worthwhile. Don't do it for anyone else. If you don't truly believe that you can be their best caregiver, then do not take this on; your remorse and feelings of inadequacy will eventually do more harm to your children than if they were in someone else's care."

## TAKE CARE OF YOURSELF.

I asked all of the women I interviewed if, at the time they were raising their children, they had time for themselves, a topic so often spoken of today. June Erickson, mother of three and grandmother of five who, with her husband, Roger, founded Erickson Marine, Inc., an award-winning marina, said oh-so-matter-of-factly in a way that made me feel guilty about ever seeking out time for myself, "It wasn't about that. You didn't think about whether you had time for yourself. You did what you had to do. If Roger needed me at the store, I was at the store." June did say, though, as I timidly pressed on, that every Friday night, she and a friend waitressed at banquets for extra money. She loved getting all dressed up and being with her friend every week—and making some money besides.

Anne Hennighausen, who I'm lucky enough to call my mother-in-law, said she always had a sense that she didn't have time to take care of herself but grew up in an era where you were Mom first, then wife. Period. That didn't leave much extra time. She was content thinking that way until the women's movement helped her realize there was more in it for her.

Reverend Mary Keen, long-time Methodist pastor, took care of herself through the seminary, as she raised her children, as she experienced divorce, and in the present. She always made herself a priority, reflected by her book group and her women's clergy support group. Periodically, she also escapes from her family (even when they were young) to a hotel for a day or two to be alone with her thoughts, books, and journals.

## MISCELLANEOUS PEARLS

"Don't be afraid to be vulnerable to your kids. It's valuable for them to see that even their parents struggle through something difficult but come out ok." Mary Dee Hicks' children learned that Mary Dee struggles and grows and learns and has changing priorities. They learned that she's resilient. Seeing their mother model those characteristics gives them permission to question and feel.

—Mary Dee Hicks

"The family unit is most important no matter what—more important than childcare, church, or school. Home is where we learn to be in the world, where we learn to love. Children's relationships with their parents is also where they learn their relationship with God. Those relationships are crucial to the welfare of the world."

—Rev. Mary Keen

"Make sure you marry someone who will do 50% of the work, someone who comes from a background of collaboration. A high-level profession cannot be maintained without a supportive partner."

—Mary Mahoney

"Question the assumptions. If you've never worked outside the home and you're feeling restless, take a class and see where it leads. If a high powered career has always been the path but doesn't feel quite right, take a sabbatical and find out why. Others will judge you and think you are selfish, but that's ok because it's what you must do to make your life the way you want it to be."

—Mary Dee Hicks

"Never forget the history of women; where we've come from in a short period of time."

—Mary Mahoney

"Be careful how you define success. It's connected to our core sense of who we are, not what we do or how much money we make. It's about discovering for ourselves our God-given gifts, His fingerprints on our lives. And it's about using those gifts for a greater good without interest in monetary compensation or power or status."

—Rev. Mary Keen

"You raise your kids to leave. Your partner stays forever. Keep each other a priority."

—June Erickson

# Bibliography

Barnett, Rosalind C. & Caryl Rivers. *She Works, He Works: How Two-Income Families are Happier, Healthier, and Better Off.* HarperCollins Publishers, Inc., 1996.

Blakely, Mary Kay. *American Mom: Motherhood, Politics, and Humble Pie.* Chapel Hill, Algonquin Books, 1994.

Bolton, Michele Kremen. *The Third Shift: Managing Hard Choices in Our Careers, Homes, and Lives as Women.* San Francisco: Jossey-Bass, 2000.

Cameron, Julia. *The Artist's Way.* New York: Penguin Putnam Inc., 1992.

Cardozo, Arlene Rossen. *Sequencing: Having It All but Not All at Once...A New Solution for Women Who Want Marriage, Career, and Family.* New York: Atheneum, 1986.

Carlson, Richard and Joseph Bailey. *Slowing Down to the Speed of Light: How to create a more peaceful, simpler life from the inside out.* San Francisco: Harper San Francisco, 1997.

Carter, Elizabeth, M.S.W. *Love, Honor & Negotiate: Making Your Marriage Work.* New York: Pocket Books, 1996.

Catalyst. *Making Work Flexible: Policy to Practice,* 1995.

Cloninger, Claire. *A Place Called Simplicity.* Eugene, OR: Harvest House Publishers, 1993.

Dyer, Traci. *Mother Voices.* Sourcebooks, 1998.

Engberg, Karen, M.D. *It's Not the Glass Ceiling, It's the Sticky Floor*. Amherst, N.Y.: Prometheus Books, 1999.

Eyer, Diane. *Mother Guilt: How Our Culture Blames Mothers for What's Wrong with Society*. New York: Times Book, 1996.

Families and Work Institute. 1998 *Business Work-Life Study: Managing the Work/Time Equation*. 1998.

Feldman, Cathy, Editor. *I Work Too: Working Wives Talk About Their Dual-Career Lives*. Blue Point Books, 1996.

Field, Christine Moriarty. *Coming Home To Raise Your Children*. Grand Rapids, MI: Fleming H. Revell, 1995.

Fox, Isabelle, Ph.D. *Being There: The Benefits Of A Stay-at-Home Parent*. Barron's Educational Series, Inc., 1996.

Friedman, Stewart D. and Jeffrey H. Greenhaus. *Work and Family—Allies or Enemies*. Oxford University Press, 2000.

Fuligni, Allison Sidle, Ellen Galinsky, and Michelle Poris. *The Impact of Parental Employment on Children*. Families and Work Institute, 1995.

Gerson, Kathleen. *Hard Choices: How Women Decide About Work, Career, and Motherhood*. Berkeley, CA: University of California Press, Ltd., 1985.

Gerzon, Mark. *Listening To Midlife: Turning Your Crisis Into A Quest*. Boston & London: Shambhala, 1996.

Hawes, Elizabeth. *Why Women Cry: Wenches With Wrenches*. Cornwall Press, 1943.

Holcomb, Betty. *Not Guilty!: The Good News About Working Mothers*. New York: Scribner, 1998.

"How Much is Enough?" *Fast Company Magazine*, July-August, 1999, p. 261.

Kaufman, Loretta and Mary Quigley. *And What Do You Do? When Women Choose To Stay Home*. Berkeley, CA: Wildcat Canyon Press, 2000.

Kelley, Linda. *Two Incomes and Still Broke?: It's Not How Much You Make But How Much You Keep*. New York: Times Books, 1996.

Krasnow, Iris. *Surrendering to Motherhood: Losing Your Mind, Finding Your Soul*. Hyperion, 1997.

Leech, Penelope. *Children First: What Society Must Do—and Is Not Doing—For Children Today*. New York: Vintage Books, 1995.

Lerner, Harriet, Ph.D. *The Mother Dance: How Children Change Your Life*. New York: Harper Collins Publishers, 1998.

Marshall, Melinda M. *Good Enough Mothers: Changing Expectations For Ourselves*. Princeton, N.J.: Kitty Colton's Petersons, 1993.

McKenna, Elizabeth Perle. *When Work Doesn't Work Anymore: Women, Work, And Identity*. New York: Delacorte Press, 1997.

Morgan, Elisa and Carol Kuykendall. *What Every Mom Needs*. Zondervan Publishing House, 1995.

Peters, Joan K. *When Mothers Work: Loving Our Children Without Sacrificing Our Selves*. Reading, MA: Addison-Wesley, 1997.

Rubenstein, Carin, Ph.D. *The Sacrificial Mother: Escaping the Trap of Self-Denial*. New York: Hyperion, 1998.

Sanders, Darcie & Martha M. Bullen. *Staying Home: From Full-Time Professional To Full-Time Parent*. Boulder, CO: Spencer and Waters, 1992.

Sheehy, Gail. *Passages: Predictable Crises of Adult Life*. New York: Bantam Books, 1976.

Shellenbarger, Sue. *Work and Family: Essays From the "Work and Family" Column* of *The Wall Street Journal*. New York: Ballantine Books, 1999.

Tessina, Tina B., Ph.D. *The 10 Smartest Decisions a Woman Can Make Before 40*. Deerfield Beach, FL: Health Communications Inc., 1998.

Thornton, James. *Chore Wars: How Households Can Share the Work and Keep the Peace*. Berkely, CA: Conari Press, 1997.

Tolliver, Cindy. *At-Home Motherhood: Making It Work for You*. Resource Publications, Inc., 1994.

Villani, Sue Lanci. *Motherhood at the Crossroads: Meeting the Challenge of a Changing Role*. New York & London: Insight Books, 1997.

*Women: The New Providers*. Whirlpool Foundation Study, Part One, by Families and Work Institute, 1995.

# Index

Notes:

This index is sorted word by word. Leading words such as "the," "a," "as," or "on" are ignored when sorting.

Abbreviations such as "23n1" indicate that information is to be found on page 23, note 1.

# About Lynn Hennighausen, M.S.

Lynn Hennighausen is the mother of three children, a writer and public speaker. She speaks at National Conferences as well as community events and gatherings.

If you are interested in having Lynn speak at your event or would like to contact her, you may reach her at:

Lynn Hennighausen, M.S.
18317 Copeland Way
Davidson, NC 28036
Lynnhenn@mediaone.net

Visit the Shades of Gray website
www.WorkandFamilyChoices.com